THE
CHINA
DREAM

THE
CHINA
DREAM

How the Aspirations of Government, Business, and People are Driving the Greatest Transformation in History

JONATHAN A. KRANE

Matt Holt Books
An Imprint of BenBella Books, Inc.
Dallas, TX

This book is designed to provide accurate and authoritative information about economics. Neither the author nor the publisher is engaged in rendering legal, accounting, or other professional services by publishing this book. If any such assistance is required, the services of a qualified financial professional should be sought. The author and publisher will not be responsible for any liability, loss, or risk incurred as a result of the use and application of any information contained in this book.

The China Dream copyright © 2022 by Jonathan A. Krane

BenBella Books, Inc.
10440 N. Central Expressway
Suite 800
Dallas, TX 75231
benbellabooks.com
Send feedback to feedback@benbellabooks.com

BenBella and *Matt Holt* are federally registered trademarks.

Printed in the United States of America
10 9 8 7 6 5 4 3 2 1

Library of Congress Control Number: 2021049865
ISBN 9781637741016
eISBN 9781637741023

Editing by Camille Cline
Copyediting by Michael Fedison
Proofreading by Sarah Vostok and Jenny Bridges
Indexing by WordCo
Text design and composition by PerfecType
Cover design by Brigid Pearson
Cover image © Shutterstock / hallojulie
Printed by Lake Book Manufacturing

Special discounts for bulk sales are available. Please contact bulkorders@benbellabooks.com.

*I want to thank the KraneShares family, who as a
team has built an incredible company.
To all my friends in China, I am very grateful to you.
And to my family, thank you for your love and support.*

CONTENTS

INTRODUCTION
Building Bridges

Growing up in Boston, I was fascinated by a place called China, which always seemed so far away. I made it to mainland China as a business student in 1998, and what I saw absolutely amazed me.

China in 1998 was worlds away from where it is today. Back then, many people traveled by bike and moped. Electricity was not available everywhere. Cities were a crowded mass of old, congested streets, temples, shantytowns, and factories. Through all of that, I saw potential. Everyone I interacted with was industrious and ambitious. Despite incredible struggles including, but certainly not limited to, the Cultural Revolution, the one-child policy, and low incomes in most of the country, I nonetheless sensed a great deal of optimism among China's people, at least those whom I was fortunate enough to meet. I saw an incredible, untapped entrepreneurial spirit.

After that trip, I would not return until 2003. I was eager to see what opportunities I could find. As a young entrepreneur, I figured that market research into China would be complicated, but that the potential was unmatched. Size, capital, and drive were the three key words that always came up whenever I was discussing the opportunities in China with potential investors and partners. I saw 1.3 billion people, a massive consumer market, and, most importantly, an intense drive to catch up with the developed world.

Today we talk of China's tremendous high-tech output and contributions to aspirational technologies such as artificial intelligence, but when I first arrived, those segments of the economy were virtually nonexistent. China had not yet developed the infrastructure or intellectual capital necessary to make advances in those sectors. At the time, most, if not all, of the country's economic and political weight was put behind manufacturing for export. Nonetheless, I could sense dynamic opportunities afoot. Despite the naysayers, especially those who warned me not to uproot my life and move to China when the country was in the middle of a viral epidemic, SARS, I was determined to move forward on China opportunities.

When I arrived in Beijing, I was truly starting at zero. Other than a few people that I had met on my previous trip, I had no leads on business opportunities, much less potential corporate and government relationships.

By some stroke of chance, I found myself sitting in the office of Poly Group, a state-owned megafirm responsible for, among other things, directing funding for entertainment and culture throughout the country. Poly Group was a behemoth of a company. The group of companies was involved in so many different businesses that I could hardly tell which was the focus of management. Though, if I had to guess, it was defense manufacturing. Poly Group handled the manufacturing of most of the equipment used by China's military and still does a great deal of that today. A particularly intimidating sector, I know, but I was not deterred by that in the slightest. Fortunately, the group was expanding to include soft businesses, like arts and entertainment, and I decided I wanted to be part of that initiative.

Poly Group was eventually quite successful at expanding into industries other than defense manufacturing. Today, they are a major player in the fine art business in China and Asia, operating a great deal of auctions in the Asian art market. Today, if you go to Poly's Beijing headquarters, you can buy a painting on one floor and a missile system on another.

While working with state-owned enterprises (or SOEs) might seem taboo to the typical American businessperson, these firms actually work synergistically with entrepreneurs. SOEs generally want to do business in a conservative manner and minimize risk. Paradoxically, this characteristic makes them the perfect match for a bold entrepreneur. I offered to take a lot of the up-front risk, and, in turn, receive a bigger share of the revenue.

I saw an opportunity in the entertainment and media space, though I could have found opportunity anywhere during this period of dramatic change, not only in the way China operated internally but also the way China dealt with the rest of the world.

Over the six years leading up to the 2008 Olympics, the government decided that it needed to open up the country to live international content, sort of a massive rehearsal before the games. Everything was needed to pull this off, from infrastructure such as concert halls to domestic marketing capacity to access to networks of foreign talent. State-owned enterprises like Poly Group would be called on to lead the charge, but they would also need foreign companies and entrepreneurs to help. Artists such as Beyoncé and the Rolling Stones already had millions of fans in China, but few fans had ever seen these performers live. David Copperfield, the Las Vegas magician, was one of the only major international acts Chinese fans had seen within the country at that time. There was clearly an intense need for more entertainment events with performers from abroad.

In 2004, I founded Emma Entertainment, an international entertainment, promotions, and ticketing company. After countless trips, meetings, fundraising activities, odd tasks, and grunt work, way too numerous to recount here, we had our first concert in Beijing featuring Whitney Houston in July 2004. It was a symbolic and surreal occurrence to have Whitney Houston come to China for the first time. The look on the faces of 25,000 people who attended the concert in Beijing gave me the impression that my team and I had helped make their dreams come true. I saw people crying at our first concert and was incredibly moved. That experience inspired me to keep moving along with this grand vision. Eventually, we hosted numerous other acts, with the Rolling Stones, Beyoncé, Eric Clapton, Celine Dion, Linkin Park, and the Backstreet Boys among our most popular headliners.

We were given two months to get a ticketing service up and running so we enlisted the services of a private label ticket site from Singapore, which helped us reach customers across China in the most efficient way possible. We were the first to bring barcode ticketing to China. Using barcodes prevents counterfeiting and cleans up the marketplace. The modest efficiency gain from the use of barcodes was only the first of many to come, and at a fever pitch.

At the time we launched Emma Entertainment in 2004, people primarily used cash to purchase physical tickets. People used cash for everything back then. It was just how the economy was run. Then we started using debit cards, and from there we went straight to mobile payments. It happened quickly, in a matter of just a few years. I could not believe the speed of technology adoption. I witnessed firsthand how this rapid transition rate completely surpassed technology adoption speeds in the United States.

Any success in business or in life grows out of struggle. While the market opportunity was promising, the challenges were real. First, the all-important task of team building was incredibly difficult. Getting a knowledgeable team on the ground in China was one thing, but getting a team of people we could trust was even more difficult. At first, I had to place blind faith in people I had just met. Eventually, Poly Group was able to connect me with the right people.

On the flip side, I had to get people to trust me when I had only just started my business and did not speak the local language. This was another place where Poly Group came through for me in a major way. They gave *me* credibility. So when anyone found out that I was partnered with Poly, they were immediately open to doing business because they knew we were legitimate or, at the very least, they knew there was a state-owned behemoth behind the operation.

Poly was a substantial partner. We also began to establish partnerships with other government entities and companies in Beijing and Shanghai, and across cities in China. In doing so, I had to gain the trust of and work closely with key partners in various provinces and cities. Each area, in turn, had its own local business climate, culture, and social dynamics. As such, I took what I would describe as a "portfolio approach" to partnerships. While it is probably always smart to diversify and have multiple partners, this is especially true when doing business in China. It is truly a mistake to take China as a monolith. The amount of diversity within the country is astonishing and always reminds me of the diversity of the United States. Contrary to what you may hear, there is a great deal of political diversity in China. While the central government is powerful, one cannot get by doing business across China without gaining the support of local centers of power as well.

I found out quickly that I had to be the trusted bridge for this whole project to work. Many international music and media companies were eager to get into China's massive market. This was especially true for live performances. At the time, the music industry was just beginning to realize that the bulk of their revenues would increasingly be sourced from selling live performances. The huge China market was incredibly tempting.

The main problem they faced was getting artists and financial backers on board due to lack of trust. In the early 2000s, there was even less information and legal reciprocity between China and the U.S. and other developed markets than there is today. Agents, clients, and their backers were hesitant to book shows in China for fear that the quality of the production and experience for audiences and artists would not be on par with developed markets. And they worried they would not be paid.

Fortunately, my partnership with Poly Group helped me smooth over these issues. Seeing that Poly Group was backed by the government and had a substantial balance sheet, agents finally had the confidence to book concerts in China through Emma Entertainment. Their entry through us was also facilitated by my team and me. And because agents had no existing connections within the market, we were granted exclusive rights to handle promotion and ticketing for these events.

I began traveling to China regularly in 2002 and sold my first business there within five years. I found success in a very short period of time, albeit with a tremendous amount of work and brute effort. I attribute this quick turnaround to the ease of doing business in China, even then. Granted, I was able to find trusted China partners early on, but to reiterate, I started with nothing.

I lived in China for a total of five years. After I had completed the sale of Emma Entertainment to Ticketmaster, I stayed on through the Beijing Olympics, where I was invited to be part of the torch-carrying ceremony.

In 2008, I reached a significant milestone in my life. My wife and I had our first child, who was born in Shanghai. Shortly after my daughter was born, we decided to move back to New York. But when I arrived in New York in 2009, China was still on my mind.

Now living in New York City, the financial capital of the world, my interest in China transformed. I became interested in the money flows between the U.S. and China. China was diversifying investment globally for the first time. China was also one of the U.S.'s largest trading partners, and numerous American firms had invested heavily in fixed assets in China. They manufactured goods at a low cost and eventually sold those goods in the U.S. This led to a great capital influx into China and contributed to the growth of the domestic economy. I wanted to develop a way for anyone to invest in the growth of the China economy.

My friends in the financial services industry told me that, at the time, ETFs were a growing trend and product type in asset management. I also decided that ETFs (Exchange Traded Funds), which create baskets of securities into listed products in specific sectors, such as China internet companies, in addition to being a "megatrend," could be an excellent tool to allow anyone to invest in China. Therefore, I wanted to pursue starting a company focused on two "megatrends": ETFs and China.

In 2013, I founded KraneShares and we launched our first ETF: the KraneShares CSI Overseas China Internet ETF, which is more commonly referred to by its ticker, KWEB. The ETF provides exposure to a basket of innovative, internet-based companies with an eye to the burgeoning tech scene in China and China's rapidly increasing internet penetration rate. Of course, the ETF has always included the storied ecommerce giants Alibaba and Tencent. In fact, we have held Alibaba's shares pretty much since its IPO (initial public offering). Through my experience, I knew that there were many other tech companies in China that were disrupting industries in myriad ways—Alibaba+, if you will. That is why our fund includes many companies beyond Alibaba and Tencent and can automatically allocate to new players as they go public and their businesses expand.

The next megatrend that inspired me and my team at KraneShares was the inclusion of Chinese stocks in MSCI's world-leading indexes. MSCI is a global leader in financial indexing, meaning that trillions of dollars of managed capital are invested based off their indexes. We anticipated that MSCI would eventually begin to track Chinese stocks listed in the mainland on the Shanghai and Shenzhen Stock Exchanges and include these stocks in MSCI global indexes. So, when they did, we were prepared with an ETF based on their index for China mainland equities and this inclusion story.

Over the years, we continued to launch new products, capturing different investment themes within China's market including health care, consumer products, clean technology, and the Belt and Road Initiative, China's massive overseas infrastructure plan. Even though U.S. and multinational corporations had been investing in China for years, China was a relatively new allocation target for asset managers and asset allocators. For this reason, we saw ourselves as, more than anything else, filling the knowledge void for U.S. and global investors about China. After all, we were the only asset management firm to focus exclusively on China. While we have now expanded our product suite to include investments outside China, mainly other emerging markets, China investing remains our specialty and continues to set us apart from the competition.

Evidently, that knowledge gap needed to be filled. Our business has grown tremendously since 2013. We now have over $15 billion in assets under management (AUM). Over the years, I have called on industry veterans from the likes of JPMorgan, Goldman Sachs, BlackRock, and Oppenheimer to join our team and help build a truly amazing business. Applying a "portfolio approach" to partners, which I had learned in China, I also had people from a variety of disciplines come and join us, including web developers and marketing professionals. Such success would not have been possible without our incredible team.

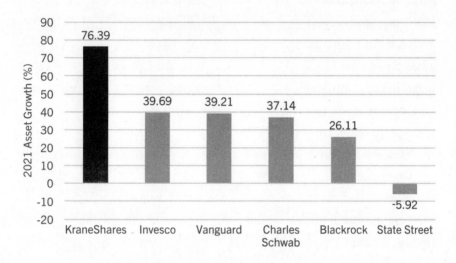

In 2017, we were fortunate enough to be acquired by China International Capital Corporation (CICC), one of China's leading investment banks, which was founded in 1995 by Morgan Stanley and China Construction Bank (CCB) representing the Chinese government. CICC had the foresight early to begin providing investment banking services within mainland China, and today CICC is a full-service investment bank and a leader in IPO/M&A advisory, private equity, wealth management, trading, research, and asset management. CICC has, in turn, provided us with invaluable support and has been an excellent partner. CICC's largest shareholder is China Investment Corporation (CIC), the $1 trillion China sovereign wealth fund.

China's amazing growth looks likely to continue virtually unabated after the COVID-19 pandemic of 2020. For one thing, the Chinese health care system is being completely modernized and revamped. For another, internet and ecommerce have flourished and grown during the crisis. We will examine this more closely in chapter ten.

At my firm, we are committed to fostering mutual understanding between the United States and China. We think that China cannot, and perhaps more importantly, should not grow in isolation, and that this growth benefits the entire world, especially the U.S. In our work and in this book, we hope to provide a balanced perspective on China's growth, while providing global investors with the necessary tools to capture this growth in their portfolios.

Our core beliefs:

- More and more Chinese companies in increasingly diverse sectors of the economy are growing because their revenues are growing. These firms continue to be undervalued by the markets.
- The opening of China's capital markets represents a tremendous opportunity for investors all over the world.
- China has become its own asset class, and, as such, an exposure to China is an important component of a well-balanced portfolio.
- We believe global institutional flows will significantly increase into China's equity and fixed income markets over the next five to ten years.
- We believe the political and economic relationship between the U.S. and China is the most important relationship of the twenty-first century.
- We believe that as China's prominence on the world stage expands, U.S. investors will need to increase their understanding and education regarding China.
- We believe China will successfully make the transition to a developed economy and eventually become the world's largest.
- Despite the competitive tension between the world's two largest economies, we believe China and the United States can coexist in

a positive and mutually beneficial manner. However, the road to prosperity and understanding will require commitments from both countries to understand each other better, including culture, goals, and visions for their respective citizens. After all, no meaningful dream is ever brought to life without hard work. Despite the immense opportunity, China faces a multitude of challenges.

These include:

▸ The demographics of an aging population and a highly educated young population going into service businesses.

▸ Overleveraging, especially in the real estate sector, which is also a consequence of having established the best transportation infrastructure the world has ever seen.

▸ Legal frameworks that are transitioning to a global platform.

▸ A changing role for foreign companies and the need for further economic opening.

Our aim is to understand China, not to change China. As one of the world's oldest civilizations, change is likely only to come from within. The great empires of Europe long tried to have a lasting influence on and exert control over China but failed at nearly every attempt. Understanding China requires forgoing many assumptions we commonly use to analyze Western societies. Nonetheless, I believe that China has much to learn from our system and that we can learn from theirs as well.

While I could go on, I will leave political debates to those more qualified to comment on them. What I want to do now is show you how the Chinese economy works on the ground, its challenges, its advantages, and why I think it is the most exciting place on Earth to do business right now.

To be honest, I am more excited now about the possibilities in China than I was when I introduced the country to Eric Clapton and the Rolling

Stones. I'm going to talk about dozens of Chinese companies, some of which you might not have heard of. While my company's funds own the shares of many of these, my mentioning them is in no way an endorsement, nor is my list anywhere near exhaustive. Think of it as an invitation to find out more about anything that catches your eye.

Another purpose is to surface a basic truth that is often lost in the daily back-and-forth over trade or currency or foreign policy. On the world stage, China isn't going anywhere, and we all need to understand more.

If my China ventures have taught me anything, it is the power of fostering reciprocal trust as well as building bridges where none existed previously. China's consumers and leaders wanted live international entertainment, and global talent was ready to go to China. But they needed a bridge. They needed someone to take that first, risky step and connect the two. The theme of building bridges continues to characterize everything I do, especially at KraneShares. With that in mind, I hope you enjoy my insights on China, why partnerships with China are important as we head toward mid-century, and how to build bridges between the world's two largest economies.

CHAPTER ONE
The China Dream

When then secretary of state Henry Kissinger and President Richard Nixon made their fabled approach to China, Chinese trade with the U.S. was less than U.S. trade with Honduras.[1]

Mao Zedong's Cultural Revolution was still fresh, and the market reforms of Deng Xiaoping were just ripening. The controlled capitalism of leaders ranging up to Xi Jinping has resulted in an explosion of per capita GDP (gross domestic product) since 1978 and a dramatic drop in poverty.[2]

In 1971, when Nixon asked Kissinger to reach out to China, the U.S. had no relationship at all with China. "We didn't know any of the Chinese leaders. We didn't know which door to knock on," Kissinger said.[3] China was one of the poorest, most isolated countries in the world, with very little trade and very little interaction with the Western world.

Today, China is the second largest economy in the world and deeply integrated into the world economy. A lot has changed since Kissinger's initial visit. By comparison to the U.S.'s relationship with China,

Kissinger said that in the early twentieth century no one would have predicted that Germany and England would go to war. Like China and the U.S., Germany and England had no major conflicts, they shared many common values and interests, and Kaiser Wilhelm and the British royal family were even related by birth. By 1914, however, Germany and England began fighting a war that neither side wanted and neither side would have predicted. Each country also never fully recovered the relative power they enjoyed prior to the war.

In the twentieth century, the American Dream became a reality based on ever-improving quality of life paired with unmatched global influence.

Americans moved from the farm to the city, welcomed immigrants seeking a better life, invented and spread the latest technologies (automobiles, telephones, radio, television), built world-class infrastructure (the Hoover Dam, the interstate highway system), helped end two devastating world wars, spread their culture all around the world, and created a standard of living never before seen.

China has grown significantly in the twenty-first century, yet still has incredible potential. If you walk down any street in Beijing, Shanghai, or a dozen other huge Chinese cities, you see everybody staring at their smartphones, just as people do in New York or Los Angeles. However, only slightly more than half the Chinese population owns one. That's a potential *additional* market of 700 million![4] And as new Chinese cities much larger than New York City spring up every year, there's a massive new market for building houses, office buildings, restaurants, highways, bridges, self-driving cars, hospitals, rail lines, high-speed trains, and, well, you get the idea. The Chinese have a dream, too, and, in their context, it might be even more ambitious.

As President Xi Jinping expressed it in a speech in Seattle in 2014, his dream as a village official in the 1960s was to enable everybody to eat meat, then in short supply.[5] This goal served as a metaphor for living a better life.

"Toward the end of the 1960s, when I was in my teens, I was sent from Beijing to work as a peasant in a small village, where I spent seven years. At that time, the villagers and I lived in earth caves and slept on earth beds. Life was very hard. There was no meat in our diet for months. I knew what the villagers wanted the most. Later, I became the village's party secretary and began to lead the villagers in production. One thing I wished most at the time was to make it possible for the villagers to eat meat to their heart's content. But it was very difficult for such a wish to come true in those years.

"At the spring festival earlier this year, I returned to the village. It was a different place now. I saw blacktop roads. Now living in houses with bricks and tiles, the villagers had internet access. Elderly folks had basic old-age care, and all villagers had medical care coverage. Children were in school. Of course, meat was readily available. This made me keenly aware that the Chinese dream is, after all, a dream of the people. We can fulfill the Chinese dream only when we link it with our people's yearning for a better life.

"What has happened in [my village] is but a microcosm of the progress China has made through reform and opening up. In a little more than three decades, we have turned China into the world's second-largest economy, lifted 1.3 billion people from a life of chronic shortage, and brought them initial prosperity and unprecedented rights and dignity."

For me, President Xi's speech encapsulates the original spirit of the China Dream and documents the transformation that occurred during his lifetime. Now, more than fifty years later, most Chinese can eat as much meat as they want—the country consumes one-quarter of the world's meat. However, that dream has morphed into much more and now aspires to make China a leader in technological innovation and to share their development model with the rest of the world. His dream envisions moving millions more people from farms into burgeoning cities, linking them all together by high-speed trains and highways designed to eventually accommodate self-driving cars, bringing electricity and fifth-generation phone service (5G) to everyone, and creating the most efficient financial ecosystem possible, virtually eliminating cash and credit card transactions in the process.

As with the American Dream realized in the twentieth century, a corollary of Xi's dream is to build roads, railways, bridges, canals, and ports from Singapore to Stockholm, Assam to Azerbaijan, all connected by the most modern communications networks, supplied by Chinese companies. Known as the Belt and Road Initiative, this effort has the potential to revolutionize transport and shipping in many regions of the world that fell outside America's purview following World War II, such as Central Asia and East Africa. And, yes, this will cause the spread of China's language and culture, just as similar efforts by the U.S. spurred the spread of American culture.

Put another way, the China Dream is to become the most vibrant, innovative, and engaged economy that it can be both for its own people and the rest of the world. The twenty-first century is shaping up to be the Chinese Century, just as the twentieth was the American Century. China's dream is on a similar path as the American Dream. It has the same dynamics: urbanization, industrialization, and innovation. The American Dream was accessible to everyone and spread hope across the country and the world. We are seeing this same hope in China.

Already, China is creating more millionaires and billionaires than anywhere else on Earth, and for many of the reasons detailed in the rest of this book.[6] You could look at it as the greatest wealth creation exercise in history, but that would just be scraping the glittery surface. The China Dream goes far deeper.

To me, no one more embodies the China Dream, nor the idea of building bridges, than Derek Yan, one of our star investment analysts, who joined KraneShares in 2015. There are millions of people with similar backgrounds in China, and understanding their stories is key to understanding the China Dream.

"No country in the world has a generational gap as wide as China's. For my family, life today is worlds away from life sixty years ago. As a lucky child, I grew up in a reformed and open China. Admittedly, I took a lot for granted and assumed that China had always been the way it is today," Derek shared with me. "However, stories from my grandpa and my father completely reshaped my views. How could a country change so much from generation to generation? After hearing those stories, I felt a deeper connection to my family history and knew that my family had witnessed one of the most significant developments in human history.

"My grandpa was born before the Communist Party won the civil war and founded the People's Republic of China in 1949. My grandpa's family was running a traditional Chinese medicine business in a small city in Jiangxi. Most of the people were using traditional Chinese medicine and herbs back then. The company was pretty profitable, though my great-grandfather wanted to settle down and raise a family. So he bought land and properties in a rural village nearby. By collecting rents, the family was able to afford a pretty decent life. However, when the new China was founded in 1949, new policies came to the quiet village. Everyone had to give up ownership of their lands and allow for those lands to be evenly distributed among the population. As a prominent landowner, my grandpa's family tried to fight against giving up their land. But their efforts landed them in prison. Eventually, the family gave up all the land but, fortunately, was able to hang on to a big house to live in.

"My grandpa was already a teenager then. Everyone had to join the socialist working group and earn 'working credits,' which could be exchanged for food and living necessities. Since my grandpa and his brother were young and hardworking, they were able to make enough credits for the family. He said life was still not bad until the year 1958, the year in which my father was born. Everyone was happy about the newborn, but then news came that every farmer would set up a 'backyard furnace,' a makeshift furnace for smelting industrial metals to be used in the Great Leap Forward industrialization push. Many lands were thus abandoned as a result, which meant that there eventually was not enough food for everyone. The family was starving along with the young child, my father. They had to work extremely hard just to scrape by and feed themselves. Things were finally getting better several years later when everyone was told to go back to the field and grow crops. My grandpa therefore believed that life could be better in the future.

"However, 1966 saw the beginning of the Cultural Revolution. Unfortunately, my father and his family had been classified as 'rich farmers' when the PRC was founded. They never thought much of the title, but when society was thrown into chaos by the Cultural Revolution, it became a derogatory term. The whole family was kicked out of their home and forced to live in a small cowshed. My great-grandpa had to wear a tall hat and kneel down in humiliation. People would gather and criticize him for his evil wealth in the past.

"My uncle was a little kid then, and at one point he became sick. My grandpa was permitted to bring him to the doctor but was unable to afford the cost of health care: equivalent to $0.20. He asked many neighbors to help, but no one dared help a 'rich farmer' family. People were afraid that a close relationship with a 'rich farmer' family could result in the same social ostracism. My uncle passed away from illness as he was never able to receive care.

"Local officials then forced my grandpa to work longer hours. The working group leader told him to cultivate the land during the freezing winter in his bare feet. Life had become as though they were in prison since the whole family was under constant surveillance. Neighbor kids would bully my father because he is from a 'rich farmer' family. Even though he was a good student, his application to high school was denied by the local government officials because they discovered my father had been reading a novel that had been deemed politically dangerous. Everyone seemed to lose hope.

"When Deng Xiaoping announced a plan to 'reform and open up' the country in 1979, the government permitted my family to return to their original house. In 1980, lands were quasi-privatized, everyone was better incentivized, and production levels rose. In 1984, my father turned twenty-six and had been growing crops for several years now. He kept hearing of all kinds of new opportunities arising from people returning to the village.

"Despite only receiving a primary school education, those politically wrong novels inspired him. He wanted to make a lot of money and become a significant figure. That was his China Dream. He used his savings to move out to a little town nearby. He bought a three-wheel truck using all the money he had left and started a logistics business. By delivering wood, coal, and even passengers, he survived in the town. For three years, he worked fourteen hours a day, seven days a week. He barely spent any money, though he felt very enriched. Through extreme saving, together with a friend, he was able to buy a small cargo ship.

"The coal and wood shipping business was booming in China at the time as the country was just beginning to build modern infrastructure. Factories needed coal for steel, and builders needed wood to build factories and homes. He saw tremendous opportunities in logistics in the city, so he sold his share of the cargo ship and bought a big truck. When he moved to the city, he heard that the government was building a railroad across the city and would be in need of timber. He participated in the bidding process and won the contract for one thousand square meters of timber in ten days at a reasonable price.

"The competitor declared the contract mission impossible for my father. In one round trip, he could only deliver ten-plus square meters; therefore, it would require one hundred trips in ten days. My father started to drive like crazy while getting only the minimum amount of sleep he needed. Even the timber suppliers were touched by his efforts and many of them volunteered to help him load his truck. He finally made it just before the deadline.

"The manager of the railroad project was impressed by his efforts and awarded him with many contracts over the years. He then expanded the team using the earnings from those contracts and finally built some wealth. Later on, he started out in the real estate business as well and moved to the city where he met my mother and got married. He achieved his China Dream after starting out as a poor farmer from a small village. In 1991, I was born in that city.

"Unlike my father and grandfather, I was fortunate enough to lead a decent life in the city and receive a proper education from K–12. Competition is fierce for college admittance in China. Although I was more interested in basketball and PC games when I was young, peer pressure always pulled me back to the books. My grandparents moved to the city and lived with me when I entered middle school. They never received much education, but they somehow still knew the value of education and encouraged me to study hard.

"Emphasizing education has been a tradition in China for thousands of years. You need to study hard, and it will make a big difference. I was even more hardworking in school because I wanted to make my parents and grandparents proud. Study time was never limited by the boundaries of the school day. In high school, it lasted from 8 AM to 10 PM and was intense the entire time. Luckily, I did well on the college entrance exam and attended a good college in China.

"Throughout my childhood, the city changed dramatically. My father's real estate business was growing very well since more and more people had begun moving to the city in search of a better life. There are 1.4 billion people in China, and around 900 million are farmers. Just like my father, moving to the city offers so many an opportunity to change their lives forever. As more people moved to the city, new business opportunities [were] created. I remember that many of my neighbors got rich from starting and working at all kinds of new businesses, from providing materials to a new fire station, to running an internet café, to running restaurants and hotels. Everyone was also constantly upgrading their houses. My parents' first apartment in the city was around three hundred square feet. They moved into a twelve-hundred-plus-square-foot apartment when I was in middle school and a three-floor villa when I was in high school.

"After attending college in Beijing, I hunted for a job in the city. I felt that there should be more opportunities in Beijing. Many of my friends had made a similar choice. They tended to settle in Beijing, Shanghai, Shenzhen, or other big cities in China. I joined the financial industry due to the potential for high pay. Most students from my college preferred to join the financial, consulting, internet, or other high-paying industries in the big city. Almost everyone received a K–12 education in China, so college is a key differentiator when applying for those jobs.

"China joined the WTO in 2002, at which point most people began to believe that they would have more opportunities if they attended a U.S. college, which was now a remote possibility. The K–12 education in China also offers English education, which makes it easier for people to keep studying English and apply for higher education abroad in English-speaking countries. After working in the financial industry for a year in Beijing, I had a similar ambition. I wanted to work in the most advanced financial industry in the world. I got an offer from a business school in Massachusetts, quit my job, and flew to the U.S. all on my own.

"In the beginning, it was a very lonely life in the U.S., but it was also exciting because everything was completely new to me. I remember my first landlord's thick Boston accent fondly. Eventually, I found that Americans are similar to Chinese people in one important way. Everyone wants to work hard and believes that they create a better life for themselves through hard work. The entrepreneurial spirit that I learned from my classmates inspired me.

"When I graduated, I joined a company with an entrepreneurial spirit that focuses on investing in China: KraneShares. Since I was born and raised in China and had seen all the miracles that happened in China, I sincerely believe that many more great companies will be built in China. The growth of China may just be the greatest opportunity for every investor in the world. I found that this would be an excellent career for me: helping global investors capture the once-in-a-lifetime opportunity that is the rise of China.

"I still WeChat with my family every week. My grandfather continues to remind me how amazing life is now compared to that when he was young. He also wants to come to the U.S. and see my life here. They were chasing the China Dream, and I am chasing my America-China Dream. I believe the U.S.–China relationship eventually will normalize since people in the two countries have so much in common. I believe there is one world, and there is one dream."

Derek's story of his family history inspires me and everyone at KraneShares. I, too, believe in one world and one dream, and that's really the central message of this book.

A study by the China Development Research Foundation and Beijing Dataway Horizon Co., published in 2019 as *The Chinese Dream of Ordinary Chinese People*, by Lu Mai, made more than one hundred case studies of the lives and aspirations of all kinds of people.[7] The authors did a lot of research on the American Dream to make comparisons but found one glaring difference: The American Dream welcomed and was partly fueled by immigrants seeking a better life from wars and oppression in Europe, Asia, or South America.

That's not the case in China, understandably, with 1.4 billion people of their own. The China Dream is really Chinese. It is grounded in traditional values including close family ties, hard work, and ambition to do better. It *has* been aided by government policies supporting and, in many cases, funding education and jobs created by infrastructure projects, but all focused on bringing more and more people into cities and thereby into the middle class. This system is often dubbed a "socialist market" economy or "controlled capitalism." For our purposes in this book, I'll rely mostly on the term *controlled capitalism*. Most people are free to try to make money as their talent and education allows, but the government also directs resources into projects and priorities it thinks will be of wide benefit.

Let's look at a few statistics that show how far the country has come in the past forty or so years:[8]

China's Development Since 1978	1978	1998	Latest
RGDP Per Capita (2011 USD, PPP Adj)	650	3,244	10,500
Share of World GDP	2%	7%	17%
Population Below the Poverty Line ($1.90/day)	88.3%	41.0%	0.5%
Life Expectancy	66	71	77
Infant Mortality Rate (per 1000 births)	53	33	6.8
Urbanization	18%	34%	61%
Literacy	70%	93%	97%
Avg Yrs of Education	4.4	6.6	7.7

Data from The World Bank. Latest data for literacy and average years of education as of 2018. Latest data for life expectancy and infant mortality rate as of 2019. Latest data for population below the poverty line as of 2016. Other data as of 2020.

Source: World Bank

One highly qualified observer of the changes in China over the past forty years is Ray Dalio, the renowned investor who runs Bridgewater Associates. He says of these figures: "To have such rates of improvements in so many areas and for so many people has made [China] the greatest economic miracle ever."[9] He says it happened this way "primarily because of the powerful combination of China's opening up and reforming following an extended period of isolation that led to a fast catching up (especially in the coastal regions of China) with the advanced developed world, the power of the Chinese culture, and its related ways of operating."

More recently, Dalio told the Caixin Summit that the outlook for the U.S. is uncertain, while China is gaining momentum, because of "the rapid development of the Chinese capital markets, the opening up of the markets to foreign investors. The relative attractiveness of them, and the underweightedness of global investors in them."[10]

The Chinese people I spotlight in this book—from ordinary folk to sudden millionaires—are united by the burning desire to live a better life and pass the fundamentals of that life on to their children. If this sounds just like America, that's because it is. Chinese people burn with passion for their families and core values the same as people everywhere. What the China Dream has done is give them hope and a clear pathway to a better life.

For instance, Nan Li grew up in Shenyang, the capital city of Liaoning province in the northeast of China, a metropolis of about five million and also the early capital of the Qing Dynasty in the seventeenth century. He was born into a military family, which was transferred to Shanghai. Nan got his master's degree in finance from Thunderbird School of Global Management in Arizona, and came to work for me after graduation. Nan eventually became my partner and we started a journey of entrepreneurship for new business, including an electric vehicle company and an urban forestry company. He's a bridge builder, too.

"My grandfather's China Dream was to see the country unify and settle down and end the turmoil that has gone through hundreds of years," Nan Li told me. "My parents were both air force officers and joined the military in their youth. As the generation of the post-'50s, they have experienced an important moment of reform after the founding of the People's Republic of China. My parents worked in the army for nearly thirty years, then they left the army, took me from Shenyang to Shanghai, and began to work as government officials.

"My parents left their comfort zone and started over in a field where the language and environment were different from before. When I was sixteen years old, I saw how my parents started from scratch when they were over forty years old, overcame obstacles step-by-step, and gained people's respect at work again. This has set an example for me to believe that I could gradually change my situation through my own efforts. I think my parents' China Dream was to have a stable country and a better and better living standard.

"Despite my parents' urging to join the military as they had, I chose to enter an ordinary university to study international economy and trade. I was in a muddle during my first two years in university because of the mediocrity of the school. But in the second half of my sophomore year, I suddenly realized that if I continued like this, maybe my life would be ruined. My grandfather didn't give up hope during the war. My parents didn't give up hope when life changed. I was still very young. Maybe I still had a chance? At that moment, I decided to try again.

"I believed hard work and persistence would change my situation like all the elders in my family had. Since then, I have studied hard and seized every opportunity to make myself better. Later, I met a visiting professor from the United States who taught strategic management in our school. With his recommendation, I chose the school where he graduated, Thunderbird School of Global Management, to study for a master's degree in finance. At Thunderbird, my friends and I founded a professional club called ThunderBanker; I participated in the ACG Cup, a case study competition among the top schools in Arizona, and won second prize; and finally I graduated with honors from there.

"After graduation, I came to New York to look for a job in finance, and finally met Jon and joined his team. For me, against the background of the times I live in, China's economy has developed rapidly step-by-step after the reform and opening up in the 1980s. One success story after another inspires everyone.

"For my generation, through hard work and persistence, the future is always full of hope. My environment growing up has given me self-confidence, tenacity, and positive characteristics. I think my China Dream is to help more people and make China and even the world a little better through efforts and innovation.

"Finally, when it comes to Sino–U.S. relations, I have learned a lot about history from the elders in my family, and I have the opportunity to directly feel the cultures of China and the United States. The relationship between China and the United States has gone from the confrontation in the past to the cooperation after Nixon's visit to China, and then to the complex relationship of competition and cooperation today.

"What I feel most deeply is not the complex international policy changes between countries, but the huge similarities between the people of the two countries. In fact, Chinese and Americans are very similar. Everyone is striving for a better life and a better future. The culture and way of life may be different, but I think behind all this are the universal common values we share. I believe that with the deepening of mutual understanding between people at any time, the relationship between the two countries will enter a new era, an era of benign competition, mutual respect, and sincere cooperation."

Nan is one of the best examples I know of building the China Dream while building bridges between the two societies. And as he says, those societies are very different. We'll explore some of these differences in the next chapter.

CHAPTER TWO
Differences That Unite

If we are to truly understand the China Dream, we must also understand how it is different from the American Dream. The China Dream is homegrown and has what people there like to call "Chinese characteristics." A lot of these characteristics—the emphasis on family and education and self-improvement and discipline—stem from the hundreds of years of isolation before the country opened up.

"The rising Chinese middle class wants a better life, a nicer home, a car, to be able to travel," Kevin Liu, an executive director and strategist for CICC in Beijing, told me recently. "We're Japan in the 1970s," a time when that country's manufacturing quality and wages began to rise, he said.[1]

One particularly Chinese characteristic, taking care of their own, manifests itself in a much-misunderstood interpretation of Chinese foreign policy. China has a huge army, but, like its Great Wall, it has mostly been used for defense. China has been invaded from the outside and has seen a great deal of warfare internally. China has expanded globally through business and economics, also known as "soft power," but rarely through military action.

Rather than a threat, the blossoming of the China Dream is an amazing opportunity. This is widely misunderstood outside the country. A Gallup poll in early 2021 showed that only 20 percent of American respondents had a very favorable or mostly favorable view of China, while 79 percent had an unfavorable view. This was by far the worst result since the poll began in 1979 just after the U.S.–China thaw, when 64 percent had a favorable view, with 25 percent negative.[2]

Too often, foreigners see doing business in China as a win-lose or us-against-them competition. There's no question there's tough competition for resources, market access, technology, and talent; many bureaucratic rules; and a legal system that is difficult for outsiders to navigate.

To do business in China successfully, you've got to respect and understand the Chinese system, not fight it. China wants its people to have a better life, just as America wants a better life for its citizens. Understand and respect the system and you can find literally millions of investment opportunities.

China actually has elections, and while these elections are not quite the same as those held in the West, they are by no means ineffective. Elections in China are held at the local level only and offer a selection of different candidates that all come from the same party. Essentially, the people pick who best to carry out the party's agenda, rather than the agenda itself.

While this might sound peculiar in the American context, it has its merits in China. Local leaders are able to inform provincial- and city-level leaders as to what the people are saying. These provincial- and city-level leaders also actually hold a significant amount of influence with the central government, which meets every five years to adopt a definitive plan for policy—this is referred to as the Five-Year Plan. Therefore, concerns can be aired, assessed, and addressed in the composition of each Five-Year Plan. That plan, however, is law once it has been written up.

That means that there is quite a lot of transparency on the part of the central government. Want to discern what the government will be doing or changing over the next five years? Simply have a look at the plan. This transparency is beneficial to business and investing as it leaves nothing regarding policy to chance.

That being said, this political difference from the Western world will always be difficult for international investors to grasp and work with. Lobbying and bartering with the government is not an option for foreigners, at least not yet. The position will always be to put the public good over the private. However, if your business will contribute to the public good, the government is more than likely to embrace it or even fund it.

As I mentioned, China has already established financial regulatory bodies analogous to those in the U.S. These bodies will be searching for insight and helping to write laws that fit their mandates over the coming years. This law-writing exercise also extends far beyond finance and into areas such as consumer protection and cybersecurity.

Also, with this great challenge comes an equally great opportunity. China's lawmakers have the chance to potentially look at the shortcomings of such regulations in the U.S. and elsewhere and create a better system. In many cases, building out legal frameworks involves starting from zero, but with a great deal of outside input. In fact, Chinese lawmakers have already taken an out-of-the-box approach to building these frameworks. In the case of consumer and trademark protection in the ecommerce space, they have begun to partner with private companies to build out a system that works for everybody.

That's because "China is in many ways our equal," Dr. Henry Kissinger told a group of KraneShares investors at a lunch in New York

City in December 2018.[3] He shared that China's leaders have a great personal investment in the country's success. They have essentially promised the Chinese people increasing prosperity in return for limited political freedom. It's not a deal we'd make in the U.S., but it does incentivize leaders to do whatever they can to keep the economy growing. That's not all that different from what American politicians try to do to win elections.

Establishing an effective means of communication can mitigate a lot of problems. Where there are effective and trusted channels of communication, conflicts and problems can be worked out. Where no such channels exist, even minor problems tend to be viewed as major strategic issues. Therefore, both sides need to encourage effective formal and informal, public and private communications.

I've seen this constantly over the past two decades working with Chinese companies. It takes honesty, openness, and a lot of in-person meetings to establish trust and then maintain it. The same is true of relationships between governments.

Currently, there appears to be a great deal of mistrust and misunderstanding on both sides. As a result, both sides need to work hard to bridge the communication gap. Despite these challenges, however, Kissinger remains confident that the U.S. and China will successfully move on from simple trade disputes.

A large part of the problem with U.S. and China relations is that each side approaches problem-solving and negotiations in very different ways. The U.S. takes on geopolitical problems one at a time as they materialize and rejoices after solving each issue. The Chinese, however, believe one set of problems is simply followed by a new, different set of problems.

U.S. and Western diplomatic theory dictate that personal relationships can shape geopolitical outcomes. However, the prevailing Chinese view is that geopolitics is mostly shaped by the objective configuration of relative strengths and weaknesses and goals of each party.

The Chinese study issues in extraordinary detail and focus on their own long-term interests. In the Chinese view, compromises only occur when they are in the long-term best interest of both parties. On the other hand, the U.S. tends to address problems one at a time and is more short-term oriented. China addresses issues holistically, perhaps another consequence of the difference between the two political systems.

This analysis does not mean that the U.S. and China always take only these paths in negotiations. But they do represent fundamentally different approaches to problem-solving and negotiations that have become evident and need to be considered. These differences can also lead to a great deal of misunderstanding and frustration on both sides. Even with different approaches, which may arise between any two nations, issues can be resolved. Understanding these differences is important to successful negotiations.

Most of my dealings with Chinese companies, especially with our partners at CICC, have been wholly professional and based on mutual respect. I always try to be aware of the circumstances of my business partners, be they state-owned or in the private sector, and I try to understand the fundamentals they need to achieve from a negotiation. I also try to understand how any given result might look to their stakeholders and the public and give as much as I can without compromising my stakeholders. I do a lot of bridge-building every day.

The Chinese have accomplished a lot in the last forty-nine years, and the Chinese leadership has every right to be proud of its achievements. Kissinger, however, does not believe China is seeking "world domination." Instead, the Chinese government believes its people will set an example the rest of the world will want to follow.

Sound familiar?

China has arrived as a world power economically, politically, and even militarily, and U.S. policymakers need to figure out how best to operate around and within China's growing spheres of influence and power. The U.S. and the West both expected that as China became more integrated into the global economy, China would evolve to look like Western countries and other developed nations. The U.S. expected that China would open up and even become more democratic, but this has not happened. In fact, evidence suggests that party control is more tightly held than ever.

Moreover, there is little in Chinese history that suggests any trajectory toward democracy. Could it happen? Possibly, but with very different rules. Henry Kissinger has noted: "Every Communist Party faces the question of what to do with the party after the victory. The Chinese Communist Party is no different."

China's Communist Party is currently trying to deal with many challenges and opportunities, including continued urbanization, globalization, the transition to a modern technology-driven economy, a rapidly aging population, making sure the pandemic doesn't come back, and, of course, the maintenance of the Communist Party's control over the country's political life.

Urbanization, globalization, and especially technology are changing how Chinese citizens view themselves and ushering in a new phase for China and the Chinese Communist Party.

I draw several lessons from Dr. Kissinger's ideas, the most important of which is: China is unique.

Contrary to conventional wisdom in the West, China is one of the easiest places on Earth to do business—you just need to know how. Controlled capitalism means government stimulus pervades much of business. It's very different from the American or European systems, and failing to recognize that difference is what has challenged several generations of foreign investors. As you'll see throughout this book, there are countless millions of ways to do business with or invest in Chinese companies and enjoy success.

One of the keys to doing business, and the main reason that foreign investment sometimes falters, is the need to understand how the Chinese government works. The Chinese government—an opaque black box to many Western observers—might also be said to be one of the most transparent governments in the world, at least in terms of knowing the details surrounding which industries and businesses will be supported by strong policies that impact the private sector. It is the main driver of the China Dream, and that dream has been laid out in detail for all to see.

As mentioned earlier, government officials put everything they want to do in a massive, publicly available document called the Five-Year Plan, the fourteenth of which was issued in 2021. We'll take a brief but illustrative look at the current document. Unlike the usually ignored Soviet Five-Year Plans under Joseph Stalin and his successors, China's plans offer invaluable specific information on what the government wants to focus on. Chinese entrepreneurs and state industries then leverage the opportunities creatively and flourish. The plan aligns everyone to focus on key goals. Throughout the book, we'll meet entrepreneurs who do just this and small and big companies that are all, in some way, part of the plan.

I've always been bothered by misinformation and misconceptions about China, which often discourage people from seeing what's really going on, and to their disadvantage puts them off from visiting or investing. Popular misconceptions about China include the false charge of currency manipulation, the myth of the Ghost City, the inaccurate mainstream consensus that the country is mired in debt that will sink its economy, and the outdated notion that China is a one-trick economy based solely on manufacturing cheap goods for export.

In fact, China's currency is no longer pegged to the dollar and hasn't been artificially suppressed; the "Ghost City," Zhengzhou, featured in a 2013 60 Minutes segment on the supposed housing bubble, now houses nine million people; the debt problem is manageable and insignificant when considered in a global context; and the services sector in China is now bigger than the manufacturing sector. In fact, a lot of this book will tell a compelling Tale of Two Chinas; the one we all think we know and the one that's real.

There's also been a fair amount of misconception about China's key foreign policy outreach, the Belt and Road Initiative. This is China's globalization initiative—a twenty-first-century Marshall Plan—that is bringing huge infrastructure projects around the world. Like the U.S. effort after WWII, China is undertaking its plan at a time that its urban population is about 60 percent, a near doubling from just twenty years ago. Just as the Marshall Plan allowed the United States to make significant investments into many foreign nations and helped U.S. companies expand globally behind that investment, so, too, does the Chinese plan. The Belt and Road Initiative is modernizing the original Silk Road at an investment of $8 trillion across the 140 countries that have officially signed up.[4] These investments will be mostly in infrastructure, through high-speed trains, ports, 5G networks, and new trade routes connecting all of these countries to China and to each other.

Pacts have been signed with dozens of countries, including Russia, Singapore, Malaysia, Italy, and Israel, for projects along the land belt, mimicking the old Silk Road, and the sea road, linking countries in Africa and the Mediterranean. This is one of the most important components of the Chinese Dream. Just as the United States did in the twentieth century, twenty-first-century China aims to share its riches and breakthroughs with the world to mutual benefit.[5]

Another key driver of China's progress—aimed at fulfilling the dream—has been homegrown equity and debt markets, as well as banks. China's bond market is now the second largest in the world. The Shanghai Stock Exchange and Shenzhen Stock Exchange combined make up the second largest equity market in the world (after only the U.S.).[6] We will look at how these markets grew, where they are going, and how businesses and investors can profit. And we'll look at how a powerful central government can transform financing and corporate fortunes overnight—exemplified by an ongoing change to pension funding that is likely to inject $2 trillion into China's equity and debt markets in the next few years.[7]

This is my business so I will go into it in some detail. A strong, open, and modern Chinese financial system is crucial not just to the China Dream, but to everybody's dream. It's also a vital—perhaps the ultimate—bridge between China and the rest of the world.

China's equity markets will also benefit from a change in how the world now views the country: The all-pervasive MSCI group, whose decisions control how a big portion of the world's money is invested, is increasing the percentage of Chinese companies in its indices, which they say could steer an additional $1 trillion to $2 trillion in foreign money to local Chinese enterprises over the next decade.

Largely because of history, as well as geography, the China Dream involves moving millions of people from the countryside to cities, and growing more cities, often up from farmland. Urbanization is the key driver of many of China's initiatives. We'll look at the four pillars of urbanization: infrastructure; health care—especially hospitals; education at all levels; and culture and leisure. We'll also trace the anatomy of a successful new city, and look closely at new megacities (Pudong, the Xiong'an New Area near Beijing, and Shenzhen) that have grown up next to existing metropolises. Each of these new megacities is expected to house more than ten million people within the next decade—Pudong and Shenzhen already do. As with other topics, we'll look at the corporate sectors benefiting—in this case cement, real estate developers, and others. The World Bank says one billion people will live in Chinese cities by 2030.[8] They will all need to be housed, clothed, fed, entertained, looked after, and moved from place to place.

To do all this, China is emphasizing technology and ecommerce. I'm going to profile a lot of Chinese companies involved in this effort. Some of them will be unknown to you, but you should at least know where to look for investment ideas. I also find each of these companies fascinating.

China has been transformed by the 5G-enabled smartphone, which has led to the growth of cashless payments and the internet. And there's much more to come. Still, only 61 percent of the population has a smartphone, compared to 79 percent in the U.S., so growth here will be spectacular.[9] A similar percentage, 64.5 percent, has access to the internet (in the U.S., it's 85.8 percent). That's more than 600 million people who don't have access. Retail web sales in China were $1.8 trillion in 2020, over four times the U.S. total for that year.[10] Nearly 25 percent of the country's $6.08 trillion in retail sales were done online in 2020. And, as we'll see in some detail, the Chinese are increasingly using their smartphones to make purchases online. Over 50 percent of ecommerce sales in China are completed via smartphone, compared to only about 35 percent in the U.S.

We'll tell the story of how this happened by looking at Alibaba, Tencent, and Baidu, which are China's versions of Amazon, Facebook, and Google, respectively, as well as other companies key to this evolution. We'll also look at how Chinese companies try to improve upon Western ideas, and how to invest in this trend.

Closely tied to new technology are high-speed trains that are now bringing the rural to the city and vice versa and connecting megacities, as well as advanced intracity trams and subways. Self-driving vehicles will be the next breakthrough, and research is proceeding on both the vehicles and the roadways necessary to accommodate them. We'll take a ride or two to show how vital this is to the China Dream.

Another clever use of technology has been the development of clean energy, instead of the long-prevalent coal, to help relieve pollution, one of the country's worst problems. Again, there are lots of interesting companies to look at. In another example of turning problems into opportunities, China is fighting its pollution problems with new sources of cleaner energy, electric and autonomous vehicles, clean factories, and rules such as limiting auto use in cities. It aims to achieve carbon neutrality by 2060.[11] Clean energy is improving the quality of life and keeping China abreast in technology. We will profile a few companies on the forefront of this.

Health care is also being transformed by technology. As the country rapidly ages, this is both a necessity and a business opportunity. This sector is growing by 12 percent a year, nearly quadruple the U.S. growth rate as millions more Chinese, mostly new to cities, gain access to sophisticated health care.[12] The COVID-19 pandemic severely tested this system, and paradoxically will lead to a rapid upgrade.

Part of the popular image outside the country is of a populace so focused on work that they never take a break. But there's a huge growth market now dedicated to getting the Chinese to take holidays and encouraging tourists go beyond the Forbidden City and Xi'an, as well as going abroad. We'll also look at the popularity of Western luxury goods in China.

Given that U.S.–China relations hinge so heavily on trade, we'll devote a chapter to a deep dive on this issue.

To close, we'll take a quick look back and forward to see where China is going. To anyone dazzled by the recent past, the future looks even more promising—the China Dream working for nearly 1.4 billion people and affecting nearly everyone else on the planet.

We'll start our journey by looking at where we are in the world's most dynamic economy, how it happened, and where it's going.

CHAPTER THREE
Where We Are

The China Dream is far from realized for millions of Chinese people, but it continues as a common aspiration. The economy is now well into a high-quality growth model being led by services and exports, even after overcoming the COVID-19 pandemic. Before I detail the many aspects of the China Dream, I want to step back and look at where the country is at the time of writing, in late 2021.[1]

As the world's second largest economy develops, the structure of its companies and capital markets will increasingly resemble those in the developed world. The China government's thirteenth Five-Year Plan (2016–2020) stressed the market allocation of resources and lowering the cost of doing business. The fourteenth Five-Year Plan (2021–2025) also prioritizes market reform.

China's reaction to the COVID outbreak is instructive as to what might lie ahead for its historically underfunded health care sector. According to 2020 World Health Organization data, China spent only $935.19 per capita on health care, compared with $11,000 in the U.S. and $6,000 in Germany.[2] That's going to change for the better.

And as we'll see in so many areas in this book, change is being driven by technology and innovation, largely by the corporate sector. During the nationwide lockdown that helped contain the virus, Chinese workers resorted to online working and Chinese students embraced online learning. Tencent's WeChat office app saw a tenfold increase in use, and Alibaba's DingTalk was used by more than 200 million people. Online retailer JD.com turned to using drones to drop packages right at people's doorsteps. A woman's video showing her using a remote-control toy car to pick up buns from a local bakery became a viral internet sensation.[3]

Indeed, telemedicine over the internet will be a major growth story. Alibaba Health had four hundred thousand users from Hubei province days after it made its service free, and Ping An's Good Doctor service has been used by ten times its previous average.

COVID-19 will almost certainly drive more investment in health care. The country was already ramping up pharmaceutical research and manufacturing, and that will accelerate not just for coronavirus vaccines and medications, but for other ailments as well. Traditional medicine is also benefiting, with demand for its products soaring.

While there is no mistaking the tragedy of this virus in China and around the world, it may plant the seeds of future benefits on how to best quarantine people to prevent a disease's spread and how to revamp health systems to prepare for future outbreaks. In China, at least, after devastation, the sprouts of both learning and decisive action were real.

Chinese consumers are upgrading to higher-end products while its industries are consolidating and moving up the value chain, not unlike what happened in the U.S. and Japan in the twentieth century as people's incomes rose. Accordingly, the financial sector in China is experiencing significant growth. Financial institutions are increasingly exerting influence over equity markets as they long have done in developed economies. In the United States, institutions own[4] approximately 80 percent of the stock market and the result is that the U.S. markets have become less influenced by short-term sentiment and are increasingly driven by long-term fundamental analysis. The same is beginning to happen in China.

China is also taking its place in the world economy. As China began to grapple with the first significant outbreak of COVID-19 in early 2020, the U.S. exported much-needed medical supplies to China, a familiar case of a developed country helping a developing one. While there are no official numbers to quantify the full extent of cooperation, reports indicate that in January and February 2020, U.S. companies shipped $58.6 million worth of ventilators, masks, and medical garments to China and the U.S. Department of State donated an additional 17.8 tons of medical equipment.[5]

But as the virus began to hit the United States, multiple leaders in China's business community spearheaded the reciprocal effort to send much-needed personal protective equipment to the U.S. In March, Alibaba cofounder and owner of the Brooklyn Nets, Joe Tsai, donated 2.6 million masks, 170,000 goggles, and 2,000 ventilators to various New York hospitals. Alibaba founder Jack Ma personally chartered a plane to deliver $1 million worth of masks and testing kits to New York.[6] Following these private individuals' efforts, China's government loosened restrictions on exporting medical supplies initially reserved for China's domestic stockpile in order to facilitate emergency shipments of medical supplies to the U.S.[7]

While the common perception is that U.S.–China relations were only strained further due to coronavirus, China and the U.S. supported each other at the government, business, and individual level throughout the pandemic. (We'll discuss other major misconceptions about China in chapter five.)[8]

In early 2021, Tin Hinane El Kadi and Sophie Zinser, experts affiliated with think tank Chatham House in the U.K., released a report showing that, despite some bumps, China's policy of exporting its locally developed COVID vaccine to Middle Eastern and North African (MENA) countries was paying off medically and politically.[9]

"China's vaccine diplomacy in MENA aligns with its broader strategy to cast itself as a global health leader.

"Over the course of 2020 China locked down its economy, focused on identifying and isolating COVID victims, mandated mask-wearing and other measures, and successfully virtually eliminated the disease. New outbreaks were met with fresh lockdowns where needed, and by the end of the year the country was back up and running.

"While the dynamic Chinese economy is difficult to pin down, here's where we viewed things at the beginning of 2021. Given that we're an investment firm, a lot of our emphasis is on factors influencing stock and bond markets. But since these are reflections of the real economy, they are worth noting for their insights as to where China is going.

"China's first-in/first-out experience with the coronavirus pandemic resulted in a robust economic rebound and stock market rally in the latter part of 2020. The MSCI China All Shares Index ended the year up 33.6%, as opposed to 18.4% for the S&P 500 Index.

"While the Western world had not experienced a pandemic in almost 100 years, China's experience with the 2003 SARS outbreak led to the development of containment policies, including quarantines, social distancing measures, and mask wearing. Each of these policies was introduced in China in January 2020, and now, China is removed from quarantine. While China's strong economic performance in 2020 will face year-over-year comparisons beginning in the second quarter of 2021, the pace of economic growth should remain robust throughout the year.

"The coronavirus pandemic had a strong, negative effect on China's economy in the first quarter of 2020 as China implemented a strict quarantine that led to a precipitous fall in GDP. Asian countries have unfortunately dealt with several pandemics over the last two decades that taught policymakers the most effective tools to control viral spread. These policy measures, which were also put into effect in several North Asian countries, such as Taiwan and Vietnam, effectively controlled coronavirus's spread in China. These controls helped China to lift its quarantine in the second half of 2020 and maintain a V-shaped economic recovery. This recovery continues today, as evidenced by economic data and the results of publicly traded companies."

The massive toll on China and other Asian countries led to a significant shortage of computer chips used by industries worldwide from television manufacturers to automakers. Partially in response, China announced increased spending on cutting-edge computer and artificial intelligence. According to Bloomberg, "Premier Li Keqiang singled out key areas in which to achieve 'major breakthroughs in core technologies,' including high-end semiconductors, operating systems, computer processors and cloud computing—areas in which American firms now hold sway. Beijing will also aim to get 56% of the country on faster fifth-generation or 5G networks. Nationwide R&D spending will increase by more than 7% annually, which 'is expected to account for a higher percentage of GDP' than during the previous five years, he added."[10]

Also, as part of the response, China implemented monetary and fiscal policy support while taking further measures, such as providing credit for businesses impacted and issuing bonds for infrastructure projects. These measures were very different from how China responded after the 2007–2009 financial crisis, when it issued large amounts of debt to stimulate the economy. This time, China's economy is apt not to suffer from a debt-induced hangover as it did then. Interest rates were not cut in 2020, which is exceedingly rare across developed and emerging market countries. China's rate environment aided the renminbi's performance versus the U.S. dollar, euro, and other major currencies. The renminbi's strength is likely to continue to benefit from its conservative interest rate policy.

We think monetary policy measures could continue to tighten to prevent the economy from overheating, probably by gently scaling back current stimulus. Chinese exports will also face a high hurdle in year-on-year comparisons in 2022, having been driven by strong demand for health care exports such as personal protective equipment (PPE) and ventilators while working from home (WFH) drove demand for computers, laptops, and iPhones. Exports of health care and WFH goods are likely to decrease in 2022 while demand for traditional exports picks up.

China provides a strong indication of what may occur globally. It is clear that the habits formed in the quarantine, such as utilizing ecommerce and food delivery, have persisted. Work from home sectors could see a post-quarantine drop in usage as schools resume in person, but largely speaking, the strong earnings of internet companies may persist. Stocks are forward-looking, so an element of China's continued economic rebound is assumed to be priced in. Future earnings will confirm the extent of China's first-in/first-out experience with coronavirus. Quality growth stocks that provide strong revenue growth and net income look to remain in investors' focus.

One catalyst for China equities is likely a reallocation of China household savings to stocks and away from housing. It is clear that policymakers would like to see housing speculation, driven by continued urbanization, play a smaller role in China's savings. (We'll talk about this more in chapters seven and eight.) The drumbeat of "housing is for living and not for speculating" is apt to continue in 2022. Even a small reallocation of China's savings could have a dramatic effect on the market.

A tailwind for foreign investors in mainland China has been the strong performance of the renminbi. A significant driver of currency performance is interest rate differentials. A factor affecting the U.S./renminbi price has been the rapid rise of the U.S. debt along with the rapid rise in the number of U.S. dollars available as exhibited by M2, a measure of liquidity in the economy. Quite simply, the renminbi's rise is driven mainly by China's stable interest rate and the devaluation of the U.S. dollar. The conditions for continued renminbi appreciation may remain in 2022.

China's bond market, along with stocks, benefited from the renminbi's performance in 2021. The reality is that Chinese government bonds provide a positive real yield, which is becoming an increasingly rare phenomenon globally. Most of foreign investors' interest has shifted from negative yielding markets such as Japan and Europe to higher-yielding China Treasury notes. Corporate bonds have seen a smaller percentage of inflows, though there is an argument that China's companies are more likely to make coupon and principal payments due to China's V-shaped economic recovery. We have been surprised by the lack of interest in corporate bonds considering the attractive yields they offer.

The pandemic may have accelerated multi-year trends. Together with the policy direction set by the Chinese government, some sectors and themes are bound to perform better than others. A subdued geopolitical environment is positive for China's A share equity market, which reacted favorably to the results of the U.S. election. The A share market is expected to grow 18 percent in 2021, driven by the 5G upgrade, health care, and consumer spending.[11] However, we believe there is a real upside potential for the A share market stemming from the possible resumption of index inclusions.

We expect the government to continue to push growth. The government wants to double GDP/income per capita by 2035. This implies an average annual growth of 4.7 percent for the next fifteen years. As a result, expecting an average GDP growth target of 5.5 percent for the next five years is not far-fetched.[12]

GDP Per Capita Growth From 1990 to 2020

Source: World Bank. Data as of 12/31/2019, retrieved on 12/31/2020.

China's internet sector benefited from COVID-19 as consumers flocked online for their daily needs. We believe this structural change will likely continue in 2022. Post-pandemic data in China suggests that internet usage will keep its momentum. Time spent on apps will likely remain at five to six hours per day in 2022. China's Generation Z has an online lifestyle that is more apparent than any previous generation, and they are becoming mainstream consumers.

In 2020, ecommerce companies saw tremendous growth in gross merchandise value (GMV): Alibaba achieved over 6 trillion RMB ($928 billion), JD over 2 trillion RMB ($309 billion), and Pinduoduo over 1 trillion RMB ($155 billion). Total China online GMV is projected to reach 12.7 trillion RMB ($1.96 trillion) in 2021.[13] Online retail sales could account for 30 percent of total retail sales, up from 24 percent pre-COVID. With increasing monthly active users (MAU) and online spending, HSBC expects the communication services sector in the FTSE China Index will contribute more than half the growth in Asia excluding Japan, with an expected growth rate of 45 percent. Many verticals may continue to digitize, and lower-tier cities (300 million to 400 million users) could continue to increase internet penetration in 2021. Community group-buying could become the next billion-dollar market in China. Community buying involves having a designated community leader who maintains a WeChat group of up to five hundred people and collectively buys and picks up for the community.

Livestreaming ecommerce has also been gaining in China and Korea. We could see community group-buying and livestreaming ecommerce driving another round of user growth and engagement for internet companies. Pinduoduo, which we'll meet later, got its start offering online group-buying and has risen to become China's second largest ecommerce company in terms of users in just five years.

In 2020, there was a rise in antitrust actions against technology giants in China (as well as the U.S. and Europe). There will be some detailed rules coming, but we believe China internet companies' core businesses are unlikely to be severely impacted as China's economy heavily depends on these services. The new regulations are likely to focus on monopolistic behaviors and exclusivity, especially with regard to payment-bound merchants and users. The antitrust actions could give smaller players a fighting chance, similar to what has happened over the years in the U.S.

This makes diversification key going forward as the whole internet pie will keep growing, but the slices may be reshuffled. As for Ant Group, a subsidiary of Alibaba, whose IPO was halted by the government in 2020, the situation seems to be more complicated as the government's endgame remains unclear. Ant Group has grown to be a self-sufficient financial ecosystem with the sourcing of funds, distribution mechanism, and clients all under one umbrella. That makes the Chinese government concerned about the potential for a "too big to fail" type of event.

China's history with reforms tells us that the regulators are tough in the beginning, but they always succeed in finding common ground that can benefit the consumer, industry, and investors. We may see big IPOs in 2022 and beyond. Many of the 174 Chinese internet "unicorns"— privately held startup companies with a value of over $1 billion—are still private. Short-form video platforms are rising stars to watch in the space. Time spent on Douyin (the Chinese version of TikTok) and Kuaishou (TikTok's main competitor in China) rose dramatically in 2020. With a maturing business model and user growth, the IPO of ByteDance (Tik-Tok's parent company) and Kuaishou will happen in 2021 or 2022. Other potential IPOs may include JD Finance, Alibaba's Cainiao logistic net-work, and others.

It's likely 2022 will be a big year for China's 5G development. China has already built over 690,000 5G base stations compared to 50,000 5G base stations in the U.S. In 2021,[14] China plans to build another 1 mil-lion 5G base stations and establish 5 million 5G stations by 2025.[15] As 5G gradually changes the internet industry's foundation, there will be more new business models that become mainstream, such as livestreaming, ecommerce, cloud gaming, augmented reality (AR), virtual reality (VR), and telehealth.

The pandemic shined a light on China's health care sector—a sector that has been in transformation for years and which we'll discuss in detail in chapter twelve. Together with the emergence of green shoots of innovations within biotech, health care companies in China had a strong year. Although the pandemic exposed some of the weaknesses of the system, it also showcased the blooming pharma industry through vaccine research and biological drug approvals. Global demand for Chinese medical devices also surged in 2020, resulting in a jump in medical exports.

Going forward, we expect China to further develop its health care infrastructure. This means more hospital beds, patient monitors and live support (PMLS) equipment, and more data integration. The healthtech industry should continue to develop and expand and make internet hospitals, telemedicine, and online pharmacies available in more provinces.

China urgently needs to clean up its environment, ranging from the pollution in Beijing and other big cities to industrial discharges into its rivers. (We'll discuss this in more detail in chapter eleven.) President Xi Jinping's speech in December 2020 during the UN Climate Ambition Summit summed up China's resolve to improve its environment. The president renewed China's commitment to the principles of the Paris Agreement and added multiple commitments to be achieved by 2030, including:[16]

- The reduction of carbon dioxide emissions per unit of GDP by 65 percent from the 2005 level (up from 60 percent)
- Increasing the share of renewables in primary energy consumption to 25 percent (up from 20 percent)
- Increasing forest stock volume by 6 billion cubic meters from 2005 levels (up from 4.5 billion)
- Increasing solar and wind capacity to 1,200GW by 2030 from the current approximate level of 455GW

This last point means that China will initiate an average of 70–80GW of new solar and wind installations per year over the next nine years. Solar and wind are the favorites in the race toward renewables as R&D and technological improvements have allowed cost to approach grid-parity with fossil fuels. Analysts believe China will overachieve these targets as it has in the previous five years.

As I write, with high hopes of the pandemic receding in many places, there are signs of economic progress happening around the world. Moreover, fields such as health care, clean technology, electric vehicles, consumer technology, and fintech seem to have experienced an inflection point in 2020. We are certainly encouraged by the return of diplomacy between the world's largest economies in 2021. Political stability and a mindset of cooperation and inclusion could certainly help spur global growth and innovation. We believe this year looks even brighter than last year, and China could serve as a model for what may occur in other countries in 2022.

American companies are increasingly relying on the China consumer as a key source of revenue growth. Even amid the pandemic, fast-food brand Popeyes opened its first store in China, and the company hopes to open 1,500 more soon. Costco plans to open seven new stores in China, and Walmart hopes to open five hundred.[17]

Under the 2020 Phase One trade agreement, China promised to increase agricultural purchases from the U.S. by nearly $40 billion, offering significant relief for farmers, many of whom are now seeing the impact from the coronavirus pandemic. (We'll look at U.S.–China trade in chapter fourteen.)

The old China was overwhelmingly defined by low internet penetration, an agricultural and manufacturing economy, a technology gap with the developed world, little concern for the environment, and limited health care services. The new China, on the other hand, is being built by massive urbanization, an expanding services economy, digitalization, technological innovation, environmental consciousness, and health consciousness. The focus of both industry and government is now on internet and ecommerce, service industries for companies and consumers, smart transportation, environmental protection, and better health care.

That's quite a change and quite an agenda. Can they do it? All evidence points to yes, but only with hard work and determination.

For me, this means there are extraordinary opportunities in China, based on what I call the "Three Ps." These are:

- *Population.* More than half a billion middle-class consumers and about 8 million new college graduates per year. (The U.S., with fewer people, graduates about 4.5 million a year.)
- *Penetration.* Rapid internet adoption that leapfrogs the Western experience (more on this in chapters nine and ten).
- *Performance.* Technology platforms springing up to serve these consumers and their valuations are likely to soar.

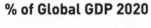

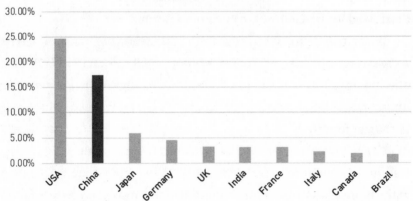

Source: The World Bank

China is the world's second largest economy in terms of the nominal value of its production of goods and services. However, according to the World Bank, it just edges out the U.S. for the top spot when this figure is adjusted for the purchasing power in each country, so-called purchasing power parity (PPP). This would have been unthinkable twenty-five years ago and unlikely even ten years ago. Many reputable economists expect China to overtake the U.S. as the world's largest economy in nominal terms within the next ten years. The pace of change is undeniable. More millionaires and billionaires are being created in China right now than anywhere else, including the U.S. The sheer speed and scale of the growth in China is arguably the greatest wealth creation episode in history.

Nearly all of China's rapid growth in the world GDP league has come from vastly increased spending on goods and services by the quickly expanding middle class. This consists of, among other things, using smartphones to buy nearly everything from produce to high-tech gadgets.

The Paris-based Organisation for Economic Co-operation and Development (OECD) says China's middle-class consumption accounts for about 13 percent of the world's spending (just ahead of the U.S. and India), and this will grow to 18 percent in the next decade.[18]

We're going to unpack a lot of these ideas and more in the pages that follow. To be sure, there have been bumps along the way of this progress, and not everything the government has backed has worked. But this system has allowed China to grow rapidly by, among other things, leapfrogging past old technologies in favor of new. That is largely why they have been able to post such stunningly rapid growth.

The fourteenth Five-Year Plan, adopted in 2021, which we'll look at in detail in the next chapter, emphasizes health care, electric vehicles, ecommerce, and cleaning up the environment. As a result, we are going

China's Emerging Middle Class

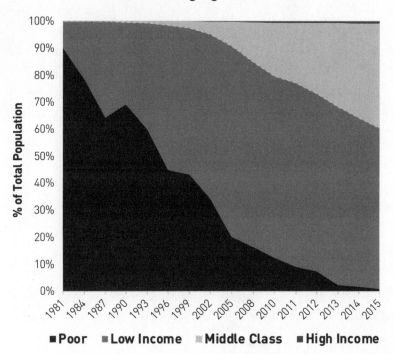

Source: CSIS China Project—PovalNet.
Data as of 12/31/2015, retrieved on 12/31/2020.

to see innovative companies emerging in each of these sectors. Previous plans had been aimed at housing and smart devices, and both took off.

The leapfrog effect has worked in four key areas:

- *Digital Payments.* Pretty much nobody uses cash in big cities anymore. China skipped over checks and credit cards and moved directly to mobile payments done with smartphones. Restaurant patrons aim their phones at QR codes (those black-and-white squares filled with squiggly lines and blocks) and the bill is automatically deducted from their bank account. The same goes for

NOT ALL CONSUMERS ARE CREATED EQUAL IN CHINA

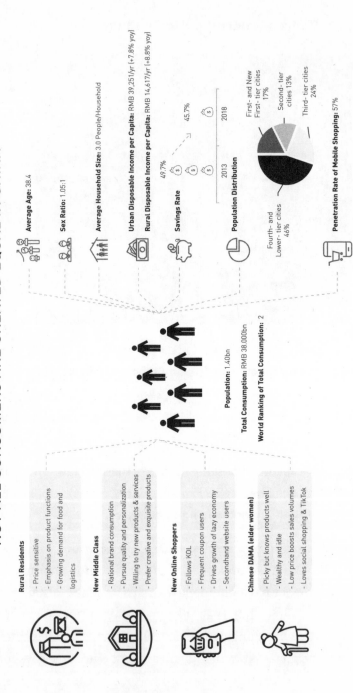

Average Age: 38.4

Sex Ratio: 1.05:1

Average Household Size: 3.0 People/Household

Urban Disposable Income per Capita: RMB 39,251/yr (+7.8% yoy)

Rural Disposable Income per Capita: RMB 14,617/yr (+8.8% yoy)

Savings Rate 49.7% 2013 → 45.7% 2018

Population Distribution

First- and New First-tier cities 17%
Second-tier cities 13%
Third-tier cities 24%
Fourth- and Lower-tier cities 46%

Penetration Rate of Mobile Shopping: 57%

Population: 1.40bn

Total Consumption: RMB 38,000bn

World Ranking of Total Consumption: 2

Rural Residents
- Price sensitive
- Emphasis on product functions
- Growing demand for food and logistics

New Middle Class
- Rational brand consumption
- Pursue quality and personalization
- Willing to try new products & services
- Prefer creative and exquisite products

New Online Shoppers
- Follows KOL
- Frequent coupon users
- Drives growth of lazy economy
- Secondhand website users

Chinese DAMA (elder women)
- Picky but knows products well
- Wealthy and idle
- Low price boosts sales volumes
- Loves social shopping & TikTok

Note: Data about "average age" in the above figure is an estimate for 2020; other data are as of 2018; the "savings rate" is calculated as: savings rate= (GDP − consumer spending)/GDP; data about "annual consumer spending" is based on total retail sales of consumer goods in 2018 (consumer spending on some services is not taken into consideration).

Source: National Bureau of Statistics of China, CEIC, Nielsen, Analysys, jiguang.cn, image.baidu.com, CICC Research

buying a cup of coffee or a soft drink from a vending machine. Vegetable sellers now have their QR codes. This was all possible because of a big leap to 5G, or fifth-generation, network technology, something we are still preparing for in the U.S.

- *Ecommerce.* Tied to that, the country moved from local markets right past big-box retailers to ecommerce. Hot new companies have grown up to deliver nearly everything on the same day or overnight, many of them the equivalents of a combination of Amazon and UPS.

- *Ride Hailing.* While it is still possible to hail a taxi in many cities, and people do still own cars, ride-sharing services like Didi, analogous to Lyft and Uber, have expanded, again with the cars summoned by smartphone.

- *Online Health Care.* Local medicine is rapidly giving way to diagnosis and prescriptions made over the smartphone, reserving hospitals for the most serious of operations and treatments. This trend was accelerated by the COVID-19 pandemic, which also increased the digitization of health records and other health data. We will discuss this more later on.

We'll also look at a lot more companies in this book, and nothing we say should be taken as a recommendation. But you might want to regard these mentions as invitations to do some research on these companies from sources you trust.

CHAPTER FOUR
Doing Business
Under the Five-Year Plan

Feng Wei's dream was to eventually make enough money to take care of his family and maybe visit the U.S. The slim, well-dressed Beijing native, now in his fifties, has accomplished both goals by doing what millions upon millions of his fellow citizens have done: He started his own business.

Mr. Feng was one of the first people I met in China, and over the years I have enjoyed getting to know him and his family and watching his success. He's an embodiment of the China Dream, as well as a genuine cultural bridge builder.

Mr. Feng's business sprang from two talents: driving and his ability to speak English. As China opened up in the 1990s, he started driving English-speaking executives around China as they sought business opportunities. Encouraged by his passengers, Mr. Feng started his own driving business, and now has a fleet of twenty-one cars. His preferred ride: a Buick SUV. "It's a comfortable car."

His business success has allowed him to realize his dream of visiting the U.S. several times. His favorite U.S. cities: New York, San Francisco, and Las Vegas.

But back home, he suffers from one of the fruits of China's and his growing prosperity: "Too many cars in Beijing," he grumbles.

According to an estimate by China's Administration for Industry and Commerce, there are around eighty million businesses in China, ranging from small firms like Mr. Feng's to giant international powerhouses like Haier.[1] (The corresponding number in the U.S., with one-fifth China's population, is around thirty-two million.)

But while the rate is lower, eighty million and growing fast is a lot of businesses and a tribute to the ease of doing business in China.

Hear me out.

Foreign firms often face what they regard as extra obstacles, though these, too, are being addressed. Like anywhere else, the majority of Chinese startups either fail or get resurrected as something else.

But look at what's happened in the past few years.

There are 174 China "unicorns," or startups that have quickly reached a valuation of $1 billion or more, many of which are still private, ranging from Ant Financial to ByteDance to Youxia Motors to Hellobike. China companies represent about a fourth of the world's 780 or so unicorns,[2] second only to American startups like Airbnb and Uber.[3]

That's in addition to well-established companies like Alibaba and Tencent and Baidu, which are among publicly traded world leaders in ecommerce and other internet-related fields that were once the almost exclusive province of U.S. Silicon Valley companies. Indeed, the fast-growing city of Shenzhen, near Hong Kong and home to many of China's tech companies, "is going to be the center of the world," according to one Chinese analyst.

Waiting in the wings are literally millions of small startups that get funding from microlenders such as Alibaba founder Jack Ma's MYbank. We'll see how this works and how important it is later.

While most of these small companies exhibit Chinese characteristics, especially those providing food or traditional Chinese medicine, many of them could be located anywhere.

A foreign national we'll call Stan works for a global company whose Beijing office, in the Soho2 building in the China business district, might as well be in the Soho neighborhood in New York City (although unlike the south of Houston neighborhood in New York, the Chinese building gets its name as a shortening of Smart Office, Home Office, according to its developers). Its main workspace is open plan, with long tables at which twentysomethings of all nationalities sit and stare at their laptops in pretty much total silence. It's also got something its New York counterpart doesn't have: a vending machine that dispenses drinks or snacks after you point your phone at it, and then charges your bank account. It's typical of hundreds of companies—homegrown and imported—seeking their niche in technology.

Over lunch at a local duck restaurant tucked just off the main grouping of skyscraper offices, not far from the CCTV tower, which is shaped like a gigantic pair of pants, Stan, who's got entrepreneurial ambitions of his own, says starting a business here is easy. "You can get all the permits you need to start up in weeks. Look at WeChat or Hellobike." At lunch, everyone pays by pointing their phones at a QR code on a plastic-covered sign at their table. No cash changes hands and no credit cards appear.

After work, Stan calls a "Didi," the Chinese equivalent of Uber, to ferry him back to his apartment. Didi is as ubiquitous here in ride-hailing as Uber and Lyft are in the U.S. From its beginnings in 2012, Didi has become the leading ride hailing company in China.

One other example of a quick and effective startup is Hellobike. Bike sharing companies sprang up in 2016 in many Chinese cities and some, arguably, grew too fast. Companies such as Ofo and Mobike overexpanded, including abroad, leaving a market opportunity for Hellobike, which is now omnipresent in small and big cities, and which is now shifting its offering to electric bikes. It's backed in part by Alibaba and Ant Financial. The company recently entered into a $145 million joint venture with Amperex Technology Co., which will allow Hellobike riders to pick up fully charged batteries.

As we've seen, by far the most important economic policy in 2021 was the fourteenth Five-Year Plan, which was drafted in November 2020 and approved in the spring of 2021.[4] Here's a bit more detail on several areas of focus:

- Raising domestic consumption will take center stage as the term *dual circulation* refers to a pivot from China's economy being focused on globalizing to now being focused on domestic demand. We believe that internet and ecommerce are the transmission engines for domestic consumption as it increasingly occurs online. Additionally, consumption-related industries such as home appliance makers that produce refrigerators, dishwashers, washing machines, dryers, and air conditioners may be beneficiaries.

- There is a renewed focus on raising technology adoption and domestic manufacturing across several subthemes such as 5G, semiconductor, digital currency, artificial intelligence, and Internet of Things (IoT). Ensuring reliable supply chains in light of U.S. technology export bans is apt to benefit domestic companies at the expense of U.S. suppliers.

- Being the world's factory has had a negative effect on the environment. Raising renewable energies such as solar and wind production while supporting electric vehicle adoption should help China meet its goal of being carbon neutral by 2060.

- Health care remains in focus as both the standard of care and the level of health care digitization will be raised in a post-COVID world. The goal is to make health care accessible, affordable, and of high quality. There will be continued support for the development of the biotechnology and healthtech industries, among others. With China's economy recovering, a big question is whether the monetary and fiscal stimulus will be pulled as the economy moves forward. The policy support we saw in 2020 was targeted to help specific impacted industries versus being a broad-based economic stimulus, as evidenced by the lack of an interest rate cut. We do not believe the proverbial "punch bowl" will be pulled until the global economy recovers, allowing China's impacted industries to fully recover.

Here are some other highlights, as reported by Bloomberg:[5]

"The government is targeting 7% annual growth in research and development spending through 2025, which would bring its total spending to 3.76 trillion yuan ($580 billion) by the end of the period. That's more than the $548 billion the U.S. spent in 2018, the most recent year for which data is available.

"China wants 65% of its population to live in towns and cities by 2025, up from 60.6% in 2019. As the population will stay roughly constant at 1.4 billion over that period, that means about 50 million people will need to move permanently from rural to urban areas over the next five years. [We'll discuss this further in chapter eight.]

"Beijing is targeting a ratio of 3.2 doctors per 1,000 people by 2025, up from 2.9 today. Due to China's vast population, that means about 420,000 extra physicians need to be trained by then. The government has a pool of more than 9 million new college graduates each year to recruit from. [See chapter twelve.]

"China is backing nuclear power as part of its drive to cut carbon emissions. The government aims to have 70 gigawatts of nuclear generation capacity by 2025 from about 50 gigawatts at the end of last year. That would equate to about 20 new reactors."

Chinese stocks enjoyed a strong 2020 following an equally robust 2019. Much attention has been given to the strength of the U.S. stock market over the last decade versus non-U.S. stock markets, particularly emerging markets. The consensus view has been that emerging market stocks are "out of favor." The reality is that investors' preference for growth companies over value companies is a global phenomenon.

Support for internet companies has recently been framed around an "Internet Plus" strategy, an action plan that seeks to drive economic growth by integration of internet technologies with manufacturing and business. The plan was first announced in 2018 by Premier Li Keqiang. In regard to Internet Plus, Premier Li stated, "I am willing to advertise for new businesses including online shopping, express delivery, and ecommerce. They have given a strong boost to employment and consumption for our country."

Additionally, the 2020 version of Singles' Day broke all records, with some $120 billion in goods sold, dwarfing the U.S.'s $20 billion on Cyber Monday and Black Friday combined.[6] Singles' Day, the world's largest online shopping holiday, happens each year on November 11 in China, which typically boosts quarterly earnings for China's ecommerce companies. (We'll take a closer look at Singles' Day in chapter ten.)

Singles' Day is a good but not unique indicator of a booming China economy. In a recent report, CICC looked at where future expansion will come:[7]

"China's GDP per capita passed the $10,000 mark for the first time in 2019. As a result of rising incomes, demand for health care, education, tourism, and high-end consumption will be boosted.

"To meet its goals, China will grow green GDP, improve resource efficiency, and accelerate the development of energy saving and environmental protection industries and develop high-end manufacturing, and emphasize innovation and foster IT, alternative energy, and other emerging industries."

As we'll discuss in greater detail, a key part of the last Five-Year Plan was moving about 100 million people (the equivalent of ten New York Cities) from rural areas to cities. The stated aim of the government is to be better able to feed, house, and raise the standard of living of its citizens in cities rather than in rural areas. That's a lot of folks moving to new homes, even for China, and to make it work the plan called for more investment (state and private) in transport networks, education, health care, energy and water supply, and telecoms and entertainment.

Furthermore, following the devastating outbreak of the COVID-19 virus in late 2019 and early 2020, Beijing decided to pump more than $1 trillion into the economy to support the development of technologies from wireless networks to artificial intelligence. Cities working with tech giants like Alibaba and Tencent will enhance 5G networks and deploy artificial intelligence to enable smart, robotics-only factories and smart cars and highways.

Kevin Liu of CICC sees the next big changes in industry, pursuing the Five-Year Plan goals, coming from those sectors increasingly funded by fresh capital arising from the opening up of the $12 trillion China market. Already, 60 percent of the companies by stock market valuation in China are consumption and technology companies, and he sees this trend increasing. In general, "new economy" companies have outperformed old economy companies in the markets in recent years, much as in the U.S. Even though these new companies have done well, there is still room for growth as they fulfill the Five-Year Plan objectives and markets open up to provide financing.

He also sees a peculiarly Chinese "characteristic" of future growth—automation—but not in the way many in the West fear. He sees robots taking over many tasks from the army of cheap laborers who made cheap products in the past, freeing up these workers for better-paying jobs, mainly in services, while the robots churn out the manufactured goods even more cheaply. He also sees new technologies, including the internet and the burgeoning delivery service industry, helping farmers. They can buy what they need and sell their crops online while super-highways and high-speed rail and eventually driverless trucks move the goods back and forth. It's already happening.

How to succeed in business in China? Start or buy a company in one of these areas and you will be likely to find access to private capital and state support.

How to succeed as an investor in China? Invest in companies that look promising in fulfilling these needs.

It's obviously not that simple. But it's almost that simple.

What we look for in the companies we put in our funds are those with category leadership and popular businesses, stable management, and visible results. We're particularly attracted to themes that follow the Five-Year Plan, such as health care, ecommerce, clean technology, and domestic consumption. We think all of these areas will continue to grow strongly and eventually give birth to global powerhouses. Here are some ideas of companies to watch for, many of which we'll return to later, as we highlighted in a report in late 2020:

Ecommerce companies continued their meteoric rise. Both JD and Alibaba saw record sales numbers during the Singles' Day shopping holiday. Meanwhile, Pinduoduo grew revenues by a whopping 89 percent and some margin improvement.

Online health care also continues to thrive and investors continue to notice the industry's pandemic-fueled upswing. In August 2019, China's government expanded coverage under its single-payer health insurance program to include online services, a foresighted move that has helped China's industry outpace online health care elsewhere this year. Even so, the industry has tremendous growth prospects as the penetration rate of online health care is still low at 5 percent.

Alibaba Health now boasts 35,000 partner medical institutions, up from 11,000 in the third quarter last year. Meanwhile, revenue from direct pharmaceutical sales rose 75.7 percent, benefiting from improved synergies with Alibaba's ecommerce ecosystem. The company also continues to expand its health care data management services, which now facilitate vaccine distribution in China.

Ping An Good Doctor also reported positive quarterly results. With only 3,700 partner institutions, the company's network is smaller than its competitor Alibaba Health. However, Good Doctor is able to distinguish itself in the marketplace, boasting a full-time staff of 1,800 highly trained medical professionals, including both specialists and general practitioners, and a self-reported user satisfaction rate of 97 percent. Good Doctor has also pioneered the use of AI consultations to provide information to its medical staff, easing their workloads.

Online real estate is a new addition to this analysis thanks to KE Holdings' initial public offering (IPO) on August 13, 2020, the largest share sale by a Chinese company on a U.S. exchange since iQiyi's IPO in 2018.

KE Holdings operates "Beike," an online real estate platform that facilitates sales, rentals, renovations, and lending. Beike also operates brick-and-mortar offices, but their key advantage lies in their online platform.

Beike has been backed by Tencent and SoftBank, which invested $800 million and $1.3 billion in the company, respectively, in 2018.

China's real estate market has come back strong following a slump due to the COVID-19 pandemic, and Beike's sales are a prime example. The company grew revenues by 87 percent year-to-year. New home sales were particularly bright, rising 105.7 percent year-to-year.

Although China's real estate brokerage market is highly competitive, Beike possesses a variety of competitive advantages, including a robust broker network, end-to-end transaction support, and a network effect that engenders extreme customer loyalty. While the company is still in its growth stage, CICC analysts expect it to make a profit for the year.

Lufax, which facilitates lending from institutions to small businesses and sells wealth management products, is an interesting fintech company with strong growth potential.[8] Unlike the smaller online lenders, Lufax benefits from the backing of Ping An Insurance, one of China's largest insurers, and profits mostly from post-origination services. Nearly 40 percent of Lufax's borrowers are sourced from Ping An's customer base, and Ping An guarantees over 90 percent of Lufax's loans. Ping An also provides Lufax access to its credit data. Lufax's business model, which is less capital-intensive than Ant Group's in that it does not originate most loans, may allow the company to avoid the regulatory scrutiny that delayed Ant's 2020 IPO. Furthermore, the company's substantial partner, Ping An Insurance, differentiates it from other, less successful online lenders.

Travel names are coming back slowly but surely. We believe these companies have been focusing more on domestic travel as opposed to international travel due to the pandemic. This could be paying off for online travel companies, among others. Notably, over 400 million Chinese traveled domestically for the Golden Week holiday in October 2020. Despite reopening, Chinese consumers cannot shake their predisposition to entertain themselves online, leading to continued growth for companies in the online gaming, livestreaming, and entertainment industries. Notably, Tencent's mobile games revenue grew by 61 percent year-on-year despite significant delays in new game launches. Meanwhile, online streaming platform Bilibili grew overall revenue by 74 percent year-on-year and added over twenty-five million users, reaching a new record.

Autos and transportation names are seeing a comeback as China's auto sales have just begun to rise after a nearly two-year slump.

Search engine Baidu at long last is seeing a pickup in ad revenue as the brick-and-mortar economy has fully reopened.

The year 2020 was a banner year for internet stocks across the globe. However, strong performance is not without risk. The U.S. administration championed a hardline approach to China, and Chinese internet companies with U.S. listings or significant business in the U.S. have come into focus recently.

While there are concerns in this area, there is also much inaccurate information and exaggerated claims. As we'll see in the next chapter, such misconceptions can have unintended consequences.

CHAPTER FIVE
Misconceptions

As long as I've been involved in China, I've encountered a lot of outdated or inaccurate information that is unfortunately often reported by some parts, though by no means the majority, of the media. Still, it can add up to a distorted view of the China Dream. I think it's important to correct the record where I can, so I've compiled the four most common misconceptions about China that I have encountered and provided my responses to them.

MISCONCEPTION 1: CHINA "BORROWS" IP

One of the most persistent myths about China is that it's great at using other countries' intellectual property, reverse engineering products, and manufacturing them cheaply, without ever providing any innovations of its own.

That view is wildly outdated. Right now, groundbreaking research is being conducted in China in quantum computing, artificial intelligence, highly efficient batteries, and virtually every other emerging industry you can think of.

The China Dream is being built by and for its people. Over the past decade, China has become a leader in research in robotics, smart manufacturing, and 5G and beyond. Shenzhen has become the world center for advanced technological manufacturing and design.

Foreign companies will play a tremendous role by injecting their talent and expertise into the country and sharing it with Chinese counterparts. This sharing of expertise is not intellectual property theft. In fact, the sharing of knowledge should be beneficial to both foreigners and the Chinese. Nonetheless, the opacity of China's legal structures has led to this criticism of Chinese firms on behalf of American business groups. But let's ignore the hype and explore the true nature of this problem.

First, although the financial world in the West views China as an "emerging market," the Chinese think of themselves as being on equal footing with Americans, the British, and other developed countries. And who can blame them? After all, their culture and civilization are arguably far older than many of the societies that have given birth to "developed economies."

The Chinese have come a long way from their historical isolation regarding Western thought and scientific achievement. China now fully acknowledges the high levels of expertise that can be sourced outside of its borders. However, China wants to ensure that its homegrown players are competitive.

The first occasion that comes to mind when thinking of foreign firms operating in China is, perhaps, Uber's loss of a China presence to Didi. Some suspect that the government was largely behind Uber's loss of its China business. However, Uber received a relatively fair deal from Didi's acquisition of its China arm. Additionally, Uber is now a stakeholder in Didi. And let's remember that Uber holds no patent for its underlying technology, even in the United States.

China is gradually allowing foreign firms to enter its market without first finding a local partner. This move is not just a loss for an overzealous policy, but a testament to the confidence China now has in its national champions and homegrown entrepreneurs.

Morgan Stanley, JPMorgan, and a handful of other American investment banks are now permitted to gain a foothold in the country without partnering with a local firm. There still exists a size barrier to entry for financial institutions, but this should be revised in time as well.

MISCONCEPTION 2: CHINA IS A "CURRENCY MANIPULATOR"

A major misconception around China widespread among U.S. investors is the idea that China is artificially suppressing the value of its currency, the renminbi (RMB), in order to make its exports more attractive. In reality, China has shifted away from a manufacturing- and export-dependent economy to one driven by domestic consumption and services. The claims of currency manipulation disregard the shift in China's economic policy over the last decade-plus.

During the 1980s through 2005, the RMB was pegged at various rates to the value of the dollar. The exchange value of the RMB compared to the dollar varied over this time, sometimes going as low as ¥8.62 to the dollar (today it's roughly ¥6.50 to $1 USD). In 2005, the RMB's value was allowed to appreciate versus the dollar, but an implicit peg was instated in the wake of the 2008 financial crisis.

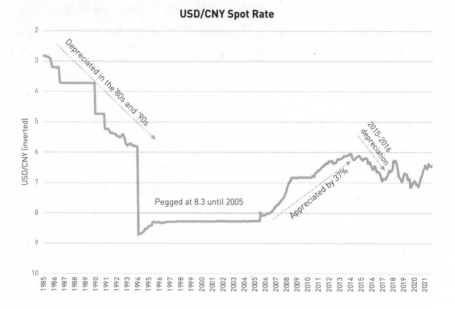

USD/CNY Spot Rate

However, in 2015, China replaced the U.S. dollar peg on the RMB with a basket of currencies comprised of China's trading partners. This new peg values the RMB more accurately against the actual trading weight of the currency. Over the last year, Chinese interest rates have fallen (though they still remain much higher than rates in the U.S.) while U.S. interest rates are expected to rise. This has caused the RMB to depreciate versus the dollar. Relative to other currencies, the RMB still looks strong, as it has appreciated versus the Japanese yen and euro due to the very low, or even negative, rates in Japan and across Europe.

China has used billions of their foreign currency reserves to slow the RMB's depreciation against a record strong dollar, a fact that runs counter to the view of it being artificially weakened. Due to the increased liberalization of the RMB, the International Monetary Fund (IMF) designated the RMB a reserve currency and included it within its Special Drawing Rights (SDR).

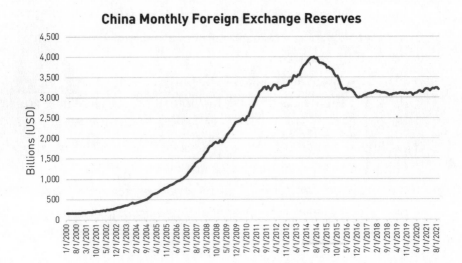

Data from Bloomberg as of 9/30/2021.

Here is a timeline:

- The RMB steadily depreciated against the dollar for much of the 1980s and 1990s, as China gained its competitive export edge.
- In 1997, a peg to the dollar was initiated at 8.3 yuan (CNY) per dollar, and this peg stayed in place until July 2005.
- Once the peg was removed in 2005, the CNY appreciated by 37 percent to reach a high of 6 RMB per dollar, which remains the recent high to this day.
- The appreciation that occurred after de-pegging aligned with China's plan to shift the economy away from an exporting economy to a consumer-led economy.
- August 2015 began a CNY depreciation cycle that lasted one-and-a-half years, with 2015 ending down 4.5 percent for the currency.
- The year 2016 saw concerns about capital flight, an economic hard landing, a banking crisis, and FX reserve depletion, leading

to a 7 percent decline. Incidentally, only a brief period of FX reserve depletion was experienced, but none of the other concerns fully materialized.

- The International Monetary Fund (IMF) launched a new Special Drawing Rights (SDR) basket including CNY on September 30, 2016.
- In July 2017, Bond Connect was established for global investors to invest into China's fixed income market directly.
- In September 2018, China implemented a new settlement system for Bond Connect to further open Chinese markets to international investors.

While the RMB may experience some depreciation in the short term, the currency is likely to remain stable in the long run. Any depreciation may be kept in check by China's strong desire to de-dollarize its trade and turn the RMB into a global reserve currency itself. CICC research predicts that, while RMB might fall against the dollar, it will remain stable compared to a broader basket of currencies. RMB declines of late have been largely the result of the currency's acting as a shock absorber for U.S. tariffs. Thus, the People's Bank of China (PBOC) is not manipulating the price of the RMB, but rather managing the economy in response to macroeconomic conditions. This parallels the behavior of central banks in nearly every developed economy.

MISCONCEPTION 3: MANUFACTURING IS THE LARGEST COMPONENT OF CHINA'S ECONOMY

China's economy is often portrayed as one dimensional, relying solely on export-driven manufacturing. In reality, due to increased urbanization and a developing consumer class, the service sector is actually now larger than the industrial sector as a percentage of China's GDP.[1] Despite the reality of China's economic composition, there continues to be undue attention to exports while the rise of domestic consumption is largely ignored.

Thirty-six financial and research firms provide an estimate of China's Manufacturing PMI, a monthly indicator of purchases made by large companies. The number of firms that track China's Non-manufacturing PMI? None.

The same goes for the Caixin China PMI Manufacturing number, which measures purchases by small and medium companies. Twenty-two firms provide an estimate for this number, while not one covers the Caixin China Services PMI.

China's role as an intermediary to the global economy should not be underestimated. China conducted $560 billion of trade in 2020 with the U.S. alone.[2] While the media often sensationalizes China, there is a growing need to go beyond the headlines to facts. It is our expectation that the opening of China's mainland equity and fixed income markets will have a dramatic impact on both active and passive investors in the years to come. Those who maintain an open mind to China may potentially benefit from all the historic changes taking place there.

MISCONCEPTION 4: CHINA HAS A SERIOUS AND GROWING DEBT PROBLEM

Many investors have historically been cautious regarding China's debt levels. However, such caution now may be more paranoid than prudent. One of the current government's main priorities has been the stemming of harmful forms of debt issuance. Furthermore, we believe that China's economy has developed to the point where it has largely outgrown the "emerging market" category. As a result of market reforms, China's risk profile has improved. Moody's now rates numerous Chinese issuers. Nonetheless, investors have not recognized the full effect of these reforms on China's risk profile and are missing out on this monumental opportunity as a result. We believe that a careful allocation to China bonds may be complementary to both equity and fixed income portfolios, especially considering the current macro environment.

As a result of de-leveraging and market reforms, China's risk profile is rapidly improving. This is evidenced by the increasing international recognition of China's bond market. China's roughly $13 trillion bond market is being gradually included in the Bloomberg Barclays Global Aggregate Index. The size of the market is such that, once fully integrated in global indexes, investment managers without China bond allocations will likely find themselves underperforming their benchmarks.

Furthermore, the market has not priced in this change, as the prices of Chinese Treasury bonds remain significantly lower than even those issued by distressed and indebted European economies such as Portugal, Italy, Greece, and Spain, which saw 2018 GDP growth of 2.8 percent, 0.8 percent, 2.6 percent, and 1.9 percent, respectively. Therefore, the risk premium on China is high compared to Europe.

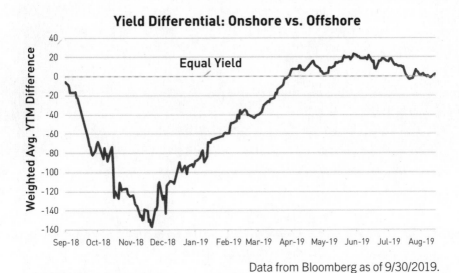

Data from Bloomberg as of 9/30/2019.

In the United States, Treasury yields reached record lows in 2020. However, China's yield curve is exhibiting a normal shape, with yields on government bonds rising steadily with maturities.

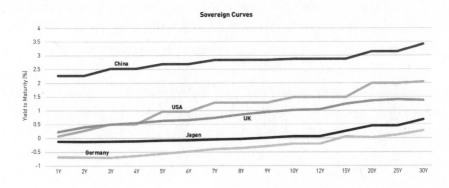

Data from Bloomberg as of 9/30/2021.

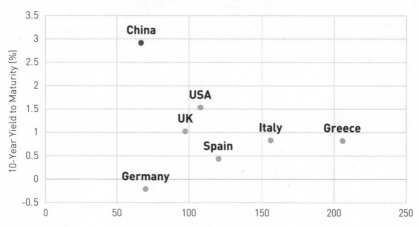

Government Bond Risk/Return

Data from Bloomberg as of 9/30/2021.

While China has been criticized for running its economy on high levels of debt, this is changing. China's government has made a concerted effort to stabilize credit in the economy. Prior to this effort, conglomerates such as HNA Group and Anbang Insurance would issue large debts in China and park the proceeds in foreign assets. Perhaps the most famous example of this behavior is Anbang Insurance's 2006 purchase of the Waldorf Astoria in New York. As a result of such practices, the firm came under direct government control last year. Likewise, some highly leveraged firms have been completely barred from borrowing money from state-run banks.

The scaling back of China's "shadow banking" industry has also been largely successful. Shadow banking is the unregulated practice by which portfolios of risky assets are sold to investors with promises of outsized returns. In November 2017, draft financial regulations were released to shore up the industry. Under the reforms, Chinese authorities merged banking and insurance regulators, and the People's Bank of China (PBOC) gained increased powers over the sanctioning and assessment of major financial institutions. These efforts are seeing results. Total social financing declined by more than 50 percent to 1.02 trillion RMB in July of this year alone from 2.26 trillion RMB in June. Official data suggests that this represents a significant pullback in "shadow banking."

Now that we've gotten these misconceptions out of the way, we can look at what's really happening in China and prepare ourselves to take advantage of it by finding great investment opportunities. But we can now also more clearly understand China's policies toward the U.S and the rest of the world, as we'll see next by looking at its main foreign policy initiative.

CHAPTER SIX
The Belt and Road Initiative

As China works domestically to build its middle class and become a leader in innovation in manufacturing, services, and the environment at home, it naturally strives to bring prosperity to its partners. In this chapter, we'll examine the Belt and Road Initiative, which is a significant globalization plan and opportunity for China to grow and share its gifts.

Like the U.S., China also has eyes on exporting many of its advances to developing countries that haven't yet made the great leap. The major instrument is an ambitious program of investment and development called Belt and Road. This is China's version of the U.S. Marshall Plan in Europe after WWII. Just as U.S. influence soared around the world in the second half of the twentieth century, so does China hope its influence will soar in the first half of the twenty-first century. The Belt and Road Initiative has been a primary focus of President Xi and the Chinese government of late. It is an extensive infrastructure project modernizing

China's ancient Silk Road trading routes established during the Han Dynasty. It is poised to reshape the twenty-first-century economy.

A massive exercise in soft power—with projected spending of $8 trillion spread over 140 countries—perhaps comparable only to the rebuilding of Europe undertaken by the United States after World War II, Belt and Road is the most important foreign policy initiative China is undertaking.

The fact is that the United States is no longer willing to provide the same level of foreign aid as it has in the past and China is willing to step in and fill the gap in terms of funding global development. Developing countries are therefore highly incentivized to work with China to seek a better life for their people. David Lin, born in Gansu province, now lives in Los Angeles and spends a lot of his time facilitating U.S. investment into China and Chinese investment into the U.S. "We saw how the U.S. became a rich country through hard work and innovation and now it's our turn to do the same," he says. Belt and Road is spreading the China Dream. It involves building roads and bridges and seaports and airports from Kolkata to Rotterdam to Moscow to Kuala Lumpur to Jakarta. This is worth billions of dollars, but the goodwill projected is priceless.

The ancient Silk Road was a network of trade routes formally established during the Han Dynasty (206 BC–AD 220). The road originated from Chang'an in the east (present-day Xi'an) and connected the Eurasian continent from China, through Central Asia, and all the way to the Mediterranean. The road was extremely important in facilitating the movement of trade, information, and culture between China, the Roman Empire, and all the regions along the route.

In June 2014, UNESCO designated the Chang'an corridor of the Silk Road as a World Heritage Site.

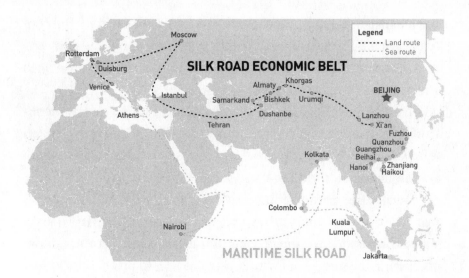

The initiative, officially unveiled by President Xi in September 2013, has two core components: an economic land-belt linking countries by land along the ancient Silk Road through Central Asia, West Asia, the Middle East, and Europe, and a maritime road linking countries by sea along the eastern coast of Africa through the Suez Canal into the Mediterranean.[1]

The key objective of the plan is to promote better connectivity, deepen linkage to improve mutual understanding, and sustain economic development in the region. This includes creating new global trade routes for China.

As we've seen, China has experienced rapid growth over the past thirty years and is now the world's second largest economy. Much of this growth historically came from its industrial sector and production of commodities, in particular coal, cement, and crude steel.

As China's economy has matured, growth in fixed investment has leveled. China must now find new channels for growth and a means by which to export its skill at industrial buildup and production. Over the past decade, China has devoted nearly 50 percent of its GDP to investment, resulting in tremendous industrial capacity that can be leveraged through the Belt and Road Initiative.

China has developed a competitive edge and gained vast experience in infrastructure development and construction activities in the last ten years. China is now the world leader in fixed asset investment, much of which is now being funneled through the initiative's channels.

The countries participating in the initiative need significant investment for development and infrastructure upgrades. The initiative seeks to create trade and investment opportunities in infrastructure and construction, providing China with a new channel to broaden its export market. China has built the world's most sophisticated transportation-related infrastructure over the last twenty years. Today, China has some of the best infrastructure construction companies and engineers in the world and the proof is in the most advanced bridges, roads, ports, high-speed railroad, and tunnels spread across China. Now China will take this expertise and export it across the Belt and Road Initiative while investing $8 trillion[2] to make it happen.

Belt and Road attempts to provide a win-win approach to satisfying the needs of the greater Asian region. The Asian Development Bank estimates that Asia and the Pacific will demand $1.7 trillion in annual infrastructure investment, amounting to as much $26 trillion by 2030.[3] China and its firms seek to meet that demand and then some.

China firms have experience conducting business along the Belt and Road routes. The countries participating are already the largest recipients of Chinese investment. Since the initiative was announced, China has signed up projects in 171 countries.[4] Contracts signed in 2019 alone totaled more than $128 billion.[5]

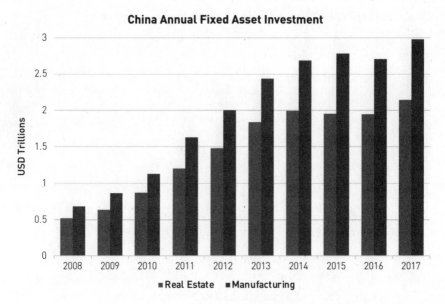

China Annual Fixed Asset Investment

Data from Bloomberg as of 12/31/2017.

Within China, the initiative has gained support from the highest levels of government and is now an official national strategy. The initiative could raise China's global economic and political influence and facilitate renminbi (RMB) internationalization. According to the People's Bank of China (PBOC), China's central bank, China has signed currency swap agreements with twenty-one nations and granted six nations Renminbi Qualified Foreign Institutional Investor (RQFII) quotas, paving the way for RMB-denominated transactions down the road.

The RMB's prevalence in global transactions is small but growing. The RMB's share of global transactions grew from 0.8 percent to 1.2 percent from 2013 to 2018, according to data from SWIFT. The premium charged to swap other currencies for RMB spiked along with that to swap U.S. dollars, Japanese yen, and euros during the coronavirus outbreak. This shows that some countries are using RMB as a reserve currency.

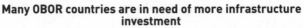

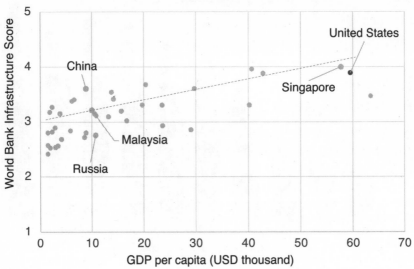

Many OBOR countries are in need of more infrastructure investment

Data from The World Bank as of 12/31/2018.

The initiative has generated strong interest from global investors and has achieved large-scale participation from countries within emerging markets.

As of the end of 2019, projected Infrastructure projects valued at over $170 billion have been completed within the scope of China's Belt and Road Initiative.

The Belt and Road Initiative currently encompasses 171 countries (including China) along the land and maritime routes, with an aggregate population of 5.9 billion and a total nominal GDP of $35 trillion, representing 79 percent of world population and 41 percent of the world's total GDP in 2018. The average per capita GDP for these countries is only $10,227, reflecting the early development stage of these countries, and strong growth potential.

Two major policy banks in China—China Development Bank (CDB) and Export-Import Bank of China (EIBC)—issued over $200 billion in loans to finance Belt and Road projects. Three major state-owned banks—Bank of China (BOC), Industrial and Commercial Bank of China (ICBC), and China Construction Bank (CCB)—have planned for a total of $527 billion in loans and equity investment for 1,012 Belt and Road–related projects based on recent estimates from the China Banking Association.

The Belt and Road Initiative isn't just transformative for countries outside China; it's also a major stimulus for certain China regions.

I had the privilege of hosting government representatives from the province of Gansu at our office in New York in 2019.[6] Gansu is adjacent to Shaanxi province, the historical starting point for the Silk Road and a major point of implementation for the Belt and Road Initiative. Our recent meeting with the Gansu government revealed how Belt and Road has ignited regional economies within China, impacting industries beyond road, rail, and maritime.

Located to the northwest of central China, Gansu's northernmost border touches Mongolia and its southern border reaches Shaanxi. Characterized by an arid climate and abundant sunshine, it is no surprise that Lanzhou, the capital of Gansu, is a sister city to Albuquerque, New Mexico. Gansu's economic heyday coincided with the original Silk Road. Today it is home to the "NASA of China," the Jiuquan Satellite Launch Center.

Prior to the announcement of Belt and Road, the Gansu economy relied on manufacturing, agriculture, and mining. However, new Belt and Road–related developments in Lanzhou include an RMB 45 billion investment (about $6 billion) in a cultural tourism project that includes three 5-star hotels and a new airline route from Kuala Lumpur to Lanzhou by AirAsia.[7] Because of Belt and Road, Gansu is evolving from an insulated regional economy into a "golden corridor," supporting Chinese industry, international trade, and cultural exchanges through tourism.

The primary purpose of the Gansu government's trip to the U.S. was to learn about companies that are focused on concepts such as big data and cloud computing to create more efficient businesses and cities. These topics may seem unrelated to Belt and Road; however, they are all subsets of what Wang Zheng Xiang, bureau director of Lanzhou Municipal Industry and Information Technology, calls the "Digital Silk Road." As Mr. Wang explained, the Digital Silk Road "is both the physical infrastructure for digital networks and the data that travels over the networks." This Digital Silk Road will coincide with the rail, road, and maritime projects of Belt and Road and establish 5G networks to enable the flow of communication along with goods and services.

Jiangsu Zhongtian Technology Co. ("ZTT") provides a great example of a Chinese company whose expertise in fiber-optic communication and power-transmission products has positioned them to implement many of Belt and Road's digital infrastructure initiatives.

In January 2019, ZTT announced the successful installation of a trans-region and cross-sea 500kV HVAC XLPE insulated submarine fiber-optic composite cable. Amid a challenging construction environment, ZTT was able to install the highest voltage cable in the world, closing a gap in the fiber-optic grid to Zhoushan Island (off mainland China). This project provides a powerful connection to Zhoushan Island and is indicative of the projects that are needed to build the Digital Silk Road.

The Chinese government hopes that the Belt and Road Initiative will accomplish the following goals: increase the competitiveness of state-owned enterprises (SOEs), augment national prestige, and offer an alternative to dollar-denominated and U.S.-led international trade. SOEs still account for a great deal of China's domestic firms, especially in the industries on which the initiative focuses (i.e., construction and raw materials). These companies have tremendous capacity and receive generous government subsidies. Opening new infrastructure markets will allow these companies to find new sources of revenue. Second, the government wishes to improve its reputation on the world stage and show that its products are of high quality and that its management techniques are effective. Third, the government wishes to create markets where international transactions are settled in RMB, thereby expanding the global use of its national currency.

Moreover, the initiative is set to potentially lift the quality of life for millions who may have been left out of the benefits of the post–World War II Bretton Woods system from the beginning or have been unable to access aid from multilateral institutions such as the IMF. In short, China is providing funding where it has been painfully scarce for a long time. Furthermore, the initiative is poised to offer unprecedented efficiency increases in the Asia-Pacific and Central Asian regions. Politics aside, from the perspective of economic empowerment, the initiative should be welcomed.

China will continue to fill the development gap. In my opinion, the best response to the initiative is to encourage transparency and find ways that U.S. businesses can become involved in Belt and Road, because there are many! Integrating places that were formerly unreachable into the global financial system will inevitably offer benefits to American businesses.

As with other sensitive issues regarding the rise of China, I am inclined to advise working constructively with the Chinese. The opportunities for American businesses presented by the initiative could be limitless if we are willing to do so. If we are not, we will not be able to benefit from China's inevitable rise.

In the next chapter, we'll look at how China is paying for all of this.

CHAPTER SEVEN
Financing Growth and Innovation

Like the dreams of owning a home, getting an education, or starting a business, the China Dream requires money. It needs startup capital and working capital for businesses, hefty government funding for infrastructure like telecom networks and high-speed railroads, and private funding for offices and houses. Everybody's dream needs money. Money comes from markets, even in a controlled capitalist system. So we're going to look at how the money to feed China's hopes is provided.

In this chapter I'm going to talk a lot about stocks and bonds and where and how these are issued and traded. This is important, governing a vast portion of our lives that many of us rarely think about. What's going on in China now will have a direct and lasting impact on all of us in the future. And it will give you a keen insight into how China's economy is developing.

I was honored to ring the closing bell at the New York Stock Exchange (NYSE) on April 16, 2019, marking five years of our flagship exchange traded fund, KraneShares Bosera MSCI China A Share, known as KBA, being listed. From the balcony above the giant bell (which you ring by pushing a button), I looked down on hundreds of traders, analysts, and investors who were gathered to learn more about investment opportunities in China.

This huge interest was gratifying, as it wasn't always there. But that is understandable considering that it has only been a few years since foreign investors were allowed into these markets. The Shanghai and Shenzhen exchanges opened in 1990 but did not allow foreign participation of any kind until 2002. Then, select investors were allowed to participate in the Qualified Foreign Institutional Investor program (QFII).

The QFII was a rigorously controlled program that let certain foreign firms buy A shares on the Shanghai and Shenzhen exchanges, companies roughly like those quoted on our NYSE, with quotas established by the China Securities Regulatory Commission (CSRC). The repatriation of assets was limited at first, but regulators have opened up more capacity recently. These days, about three hundred foreign institutions have investments of more than $100 billion under the QFII program. That's something, but in a $12 trillion economy, it's far from everything. (Our KBA fund owns mainly China "blue chips" such as liquor giant Kweichow Moutai Co., Ping An Insurance Group, and China Merchants Bank.)

In 2014, Shanghai-Hong Kong Stock Connect was launched to allow a two-way trading link between the Shanghai and Hong Kong exchanges. This was the first time that foreign investors could buy China A shares directly on the Shanghai Stock Exchange through trading accounts in Hong Kong. A similar connect program was opened for Shenzhen-traded stocks just a few years ago, in 2016.

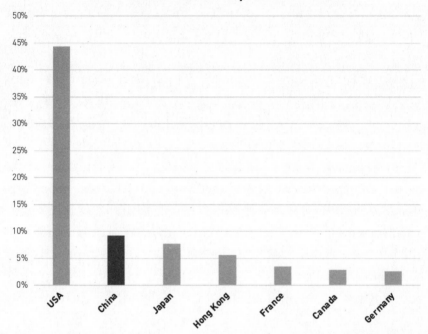

Share of World Market Capitalization in 2018

Source: Bloomberg as of 6/30/2020.

There's a lot of catching up to do. China is the world's second-biggest economy after the U.S., but its market capitalization—the value of all its listed companies—was $12.2 trillion in 2020.[1] The U.S. accounted for about $40.7 trillion. These figures will surely shift from the U.S. and other developed markets to China in the years ahead. The reasons why this shift is inevitable are laid out in subsequent chapters. The companies leading the way in health care, the internet, artificial intelligence, electric vehicles, high-speed trains, green technologies, and more will all be attractive investments for years to come.

Market opening will draw more money their way, the same way markets funded the growth of Ford, General Electric, AT&T, and others during the rise of the American Century. Indeed, roughly two hundred Chinese companies are listed on U.S. stock exchanges, mostly on the technology-oriented NASDAQ, and as Chinese companies develop, that number should grow.

As if that impulse were not enough, China's government has recently stepped up its funding for state pensions as the population ages. By some estimates, it will pump an additional $2 trillion into these funds in the next few years, all of which will be invested in stocks and bonds.

If the investing habits of Zhang Dalong from Changchun in the northeastern province of Jilin are anything to go by, the investment base should prove stable for the long term. A basketball star in the air force, Zhang made a few prescient stock market investments starting in 1995 and has never looked back. "The core value of China is family," he says. "Your motivation is to work hard and overcome obstacles in order to support your family." He still owns the first stock he ever bought twenty-five years ago, a railroad company, and he pretty much buys and holds. "Do your research, like the stocks you buy, and hold them," he says. Warren Buffett would be proud.

Opening the financial markets in a measured way is also a priority in the 2021 Five-Year Plan. Already, in July 2019, the government encouraged investments in bonds that financial institutions trade among themselves. Such investment vehicles are common and relatively safe in the U.S., and an important way banks ensure they have enough money to lend at any given time. But these bonds have historically been unavailable to foreigners in China. The government is also allowing international ratings companies, such as Standard & Poor's and Moody's, to rate these bonds, so investors have an idea of the risk involved. Moody's now rates nearly fifty quasi-sovereign issuers in China and S&P Global Ratings assigned a AAA rating in July 2019 to bonds of ICBC Financial Leasing Company, a unit of the giant Industrial and Commercial Bank of China. S&P does this every day all over the world, but this was the agency's very first rating of a Chinese bond.

Also, in 2019, the Shanghai Stock Exchange began cross-listing some of its stocks in London to attract more international investors. Huatai Securities was the first to cross-list in London and raised nearly $2 billion.

To compete with NASDAQ in the US, the Shanghai Stock Exchange also opened a so-called technology board, the STAR Market, which began trading fast-growing companies like Suzhou HYC Technology Co., an equipment testing company. This market is expected to rival Shenzhen as the place to trade technology stocks, as well as offering Chinese companies a local alternative to NASDAQ or Hong Kong to raise money.

Here's a summary of a report we did on STAR:[2]

"As China has quickly become a world leader in innovation, the Shanghai Stock Exchange developed the STAR Market to promote China's high growth publicly-listed science and technology companies. The STAR Market includes companies from industries such as new-generation information technology, biomedicine, new energy, and environmental protection.

"Since its establishment in July 2019, the STAR Market has become one of the largest IPO markets globally and a premier listing venue for prominent Chinese 'unicorns'—a privately held startup company with a value of over $1 billion. In just over a year, the STAR Market facilitated 200 companies to raise $44 billion. The increase in fund-raising activity on China exchanges last year is mainly attributable to new STAR Market listings, which accounted for 47% of capital raised across China's Mainland A-Share market in 2020."

And as mentioned in chapter two, the world's pension funds can now safely invest in China, to the benefit of their investors who will see higher returns. China's companies are now able to tap a worldwide massive pool of capital. The process began in 2016, when the International Monetary Fund recognized the yuan as a reserve currency. It is now part of the basket of Special Drawing Rights (SDR) currencies, an indication, in the currency world, that you've arrived.

As a constituent of the SDR basket, the yuan is available to IMF member states to be used for the repayment of IMF loans and the receipt of IMF loans and allocations. The decision also means that the benchmark yield on the three-month China Treasury bond will be included in the SDR Interest Rate, the base rate the IMF charges on loans to member states and vice versa.

And as the economy has opened, the RMB has appreciated from a relatively low rate of 8.3 to the dollar from 1994 until 2005 to about 6.5 to the dollar. Also, China's export boom has earned the country nearly $3 trillion in foreign currency reserves, $1 trillion of which is invested in U.S. Treasuries.

Recently, MSCI, the high standard of indexing, and Bloomberg began a gradual process of including mainland China equities and bonds in their indexes, which means more global investors and funds will buy these securities and include them in their offerings to investors. More buying means higher prices.

This is a big deal. Hundreds of billions more dollars are likely to flow into these markets and companies over the next five years, one of the biggest asset transfers in history. More than $14 trillion in stocks are benchmarked to MSCI indexes, $1.3 trillion worth in the MSCI Emerging Markets Index, where China's stocks reside. Ninety-nine of the top one hundred global investment managers use them, and 94 percent of U.S. pension fund assets are benchmarked to MSCI indexes. The moves to give China shares a bigger exposure in these indexes means an extra allocation of $1 trillion to $2 trillion in China's listed companies. It also gives U.S. investors a way to buy into the huge growth that's coming and will be reflected in the shares of these companies.

This is also long overdue. China has never pulled its weight in these indexes, which, understandably, tip heavily to the U.S. As of the end of 2020, U.S. stocks accounted for more than 50 percent of the market capitalization in the MSCI All Country World Index, with China at about 5 percent, behind Japan and the U.K. When adjusted for GDP, China is second behind the U.S., but still underweighted.

Still, these moves taken together mean that investments in Chinese companies have become as routine as buying a few hundred shares of IBM. Interest in China A shares is likely to continue its upward trend. The China A share market, roughly equivalent to our NYSE, and with more than five thousand companies working toward national objectives, is simply too big to ignore.

We launched our first U.S.-listed China Exchange Traded Fund (ETF) on the NYSE in 2013 focused on the China Internet sector (KWEB) and followed it up with the KBA fund in March 2014. Since then, we've watched as China went global, with most central banks holding some Chinese cash as reserves, and foreign investors clamoring to get into safe and potentially lucrative investments. We later added more funds as China continued to manifest itself as a highly attractive place to invest.

And, as with many other sectors of the new economy, China is right at the head of the pack. Jack Ma, the founder and CEO of tech giant Alibaba, started a company called MYbank to make small but crucial loans to the owners of very small businesses who apply via their phones. These companies range from neighborhood vegetable stalls to entrepreneurs who are sure they are the next Steve Jobs or Bill Gates. The computers take over, check credit worthiness and an array of other information available online, and approve the loans, which show up in the applicants' accounts. Payback rates are nearly 100 percent.

According to a Bloomberg article from July 2019, in its first four years of operation MyBank had loaned $290 billion to about sixteen million small companies.[3] Its success has spurred competition from Tencent Holdings Ltd., Ping An Insurance Group Co., and state-owned China Construction Bank.

MYbank and the payments processor for Alibaba's marketplace were spun off from Alibaba together as Ant Financial in 2014. Now known as Ant Group, the company is valued at north of $200 billion.

Investment opportunities will continue to open, something I find endlessly exciting. In fact, one of the biggest ongoing opportunities opening up is in Chinese bonds, a subject some people find boring, but I find thrilling.

In the U.S., the bond market is, in fact, four times larger than the stock market, though it gets much less attention from the average investor. So, too, in China.

China's $15.8 trillion bond market ranks second only behind that of the U.S. ($45.6 trillion). Having just opened to global investment, China's bond market has limited foreign investors. But that's changing, and fast. At the end of 2018, the Bloomberg Barclays Emerging Market Local Currency Government Bond Index did not include China. However, as of June 2020, China was the index's largest constituent country, representing over one-third of the index! The People's Bank of China (PBOC), China's central bank, estimates that 15 percent of the onshore China market could become foreign owned. This is compared to Japan's bond market, which, despite low yields, is highly internationalized. About 8 percent of Japan's bond market is foreign owned. Increased foreign investment should also help instill market discipline.

It's worth spending some time on China's bond market to understand how it will finance the China Dream.

China's bond market really took off in the '80s. At first, only primary issues of government bonds could be traded and invested in. However, in 1988, a secondary market was established for government bonds, and that market then gradually began to include corporate issues during Deng Xiaoping's policy program of "Reform and Opening Up."

In 2001, a system for market makers was established, leading to a dramatic increase in liquidity. As with the stock markets, in 2002, foreigners were first allowed to enter the market through the QFII and RQFII (Renminbi Qualified Foreign Institutional Investor) programs. Under these programs, foreigners were required to register with China's regulators and submit a detailed accounting of their investments to authorities. Limits were also imposed on foreign exchange. However, in 2017, the Bond Connect program was established, enabling foreign investors with Hong Kong accounts to trade in Chinese bonds, of both the government and corporate variety, with very few restrictions. Many experts believe that, as a result, foreign investment in Chinese bonds will grow exponentially in the years to come.

In mid-2021, China's interest rate target was 3.25 percent, and GDP growth was projected at 8.5 percent, a bounce-back from a much lower rate in 2020. The yield on a ten-year China treasury is, at the time of writing, around 3 percent. China's central bank did not ease nearly as much as many developed central banks during the COVID-19 crisis. Despite being a planned economy, China, in this instance appears to instill more market discipline than many "developed" countries, at least in terms of monetary policy.

This has been reflected in the price performance of China's currency, the renminbi, over the past few years. The currency was remarkably stable during 2020, a tumultuous year for financial markets, appreciating by about 5 percent. Furthermore, China maintains considerable foreign exchange (FX) reserves that work as an insurance policy against runaway depreciation. China's FX reserves are currently worth over $3 trillion.

As discussed in chapter five, China does not "manipulate" its currency to make its exports more competitive. The PBOC responds with policy in response to macroeconomic conditions just like every central bank on the planet. In fact, the renminbi is no longer pegged to the dollar at a fixed exchange rate. Furthermore, the central bank's conservative monetary policy of late suggests that the country's leaders are happy to see the currency appreciate versus the dollar. Depreciation may actually be kept in check by China's strong desire to unlink its trade from the U.S. dollar and enhance the RMB as a widely used global reserve currency.

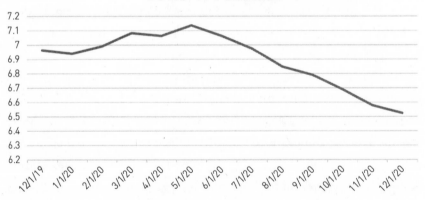

China's Currency Appreciated in 2020 Amid the COVID-19 Pandemic

Source: Bloomberg as of 12/31/2020.

This reality, coupled with China's tremendous growth rate that does not yet show signs of slowing, will likely continue to entice foreign investment in its bond market.

In turn, more money flowing into China from abroad lessens pressure on local sources, both state-backed and private, for the funds needed for all those new companies we talked about in chapter four, as well as for infrastructure, innovation, and health spending, which we will discuss in chapters ten, eleven, and twelve. It represents a long-needed and very positive development.

While China has been criticized for running its economy on high levels of debt, this is cushioned by China's high level of household savings. When looking at China's economy as a balance sheet, the high savings rate suggests China's economy is far from overleveraged. Additionally, China's government has made a concerted effort of late to stabilize credit expansion in the economy. And, considering the high level of U.S. debt and that of other developed countries in response to the COVID-19 pandemic, China's balance sheet is extremely attractive compared to that of the U.S. and other developed countries.

In November 2017, China's government drafted new financial regulations that have been likened to the Dodd-Frank banking regulations instituted in the United States following the 2008 global financial crisis. As part of these reforms, the authorities merged banking and insurance regulators, and the PBOC gained increased powers over the sanctioning and assessment of major financial institutions.

All of these factors have led to a significant improvement in China's risk profile over the past decade. This is perhaps best demonstrated by the fact that high-yield corporate default rates in China finished off 2019 at a low level compared to the rest of the emerging world. In July 2019, Moody's affirmed the central government's rating as an A1 sovereign with a stable outlook. This places China's sovereign rating on par with Japan's and higher than many Asian governments.

Not only are China's financial markets well equipped to fuel growth and innovation, but the financial markets themselves are also sources of great innovation and growth. Companies and banks are mirroring the innovation they are helping to fund. Financial technology is going to be one of the most significant and fast-growing sectors in the next decade, combining traditional banking tasks, especially loaning money, with artificial intelligence to remove some of the last remaining roadblocks to faster growth.

As with most things in China, financial technology and innovation only spur more financial technology and innovation. Given the vast scale, testing thousands of ideas on millions of people winds up serving billions of people and fostering even more new ideas. We'll see in the next chapter many of these ideas being applied to rapid urbanization and smart cities.

CHAPTER EIGHT
Urbanization, Megacities, and Smart Cities

The American Dream was realized in the twentieth century as people swarmed across the continent, often leaving farms to move to cities and suburbs from coast to coast. The China Dream is being realized the same way, only a lot faster.

In twenty years, Beijing has grown from a supercity of 13.6 million people to a megacity of 21.5 million, expanded outward in all directions, is surrounded by seven ring roads, and hosts a completely new business district full of soaring office skyscrapers developed where old houses and shops used to be situated. The city seems to get bigger every time I visit. According to one resident who often drives out from the central business district: "After you leave Beijing, there's more Beijing."

Over the next fifteen years, a brand-new city on Beijing's outskirts, called Xiong'an, will house millions more people moving in from rural areas or out from the center.

Shanghai already has its new nearby twin, Pudong, which basically became a new Manhattan from nothing in ten years. In the south,

Shenzhen has sprung up and nearly eclipsed Hong Kong, just to its south, hosting the highest concentration of high-tech manufacturing companies in the country and the world, leaving Silicon Valley in its wake. From three hundred thousand people generally living in hovels in the shadow of Hong Kong in 1980, Shenzhen now boasts eleven million people, modern factories, gleaming skyscrapers, and a gross domestic product about equal to Argentina's. Counting Hong Kong and its surrounding areas, the sixty-five-million-strong Shenzhen metropolitan area may be the biggest in the world.

This is all being done according to the plan, and it's far from over.

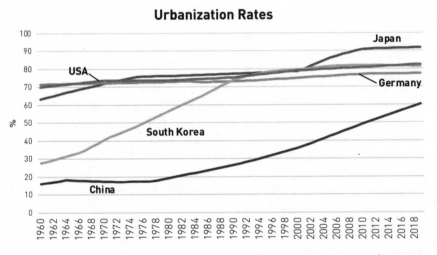

Urbanization Rates

Source: World Bank as of 12/31/2019.

That steep dark gray line at the bottom represents hundreds of millions of people moving off farms and into cities in just the last two generations. China's urbanization rate soared from 20 percent to more than 50 percent in forty years and is headed toward 75 percent in the next decade. By contrast, it took the U.S. four generations to move from 20 percent to 50 percent of its population in cities.

It's crucial to note that the U.S. hit 60 percent urbanization just after World War II, and just as it was becoming a world power, using the Marshall Plan to aid Europe's postwar recovery and spread its influence all over the world. China is at the same point of urbanization now, and, as noted previously, is exerting its influence on world development through the Belt and Road Initiative. The timing is not coincidental.

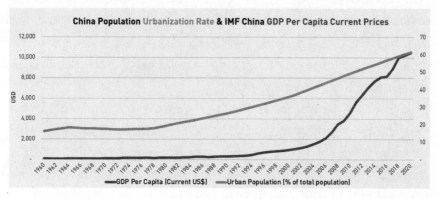

Data from World Bank as of 12/31/2020.

China's urbanization pretty closely follows what happened in the U.S., albeit much faster in China, for reasons we'll soon see. In the U.S. of all those "amber waves of grain," when "America the Beautiful" was written in 1895, the country was about 80 percent rural and 20 percent urban. Those numbers switched in 125 years. As they were invented and perfected, factories, automobiles, the proliferation of universities, air travel, electrification, hydroelectric power, and telecommunications gradually fueled the American Dream, turning the continent into an economic powerhouse. It just took a while.

All of the above and more is happening to create the China Dream, and all in real time. Urbanization in China only started picking up steam in the 1980s, after all those things Americans had to wait for were already in full bloom. China could borrow or reinvent most of the technology, skip some generations of telecommunications, for example, and seamlessly blend in the latest advances in artificial intelligence and biotechnology, some of which it invented at home.

And the transformation is not yet complete. Even with the huge influx of people from rural areas to massive cities, China's overall urbanization rate of 60 percent trails Germany, South Korea, and the U.S., all of which are currently around 80 percent, and Japan, which is closer to 90 percent. Trendlines suggest China will catch up in the next two decades, which means another huge wave of people moving to cities, some of which don't even exist yet.

Obviously, the history and political systems in the U.S. and China were and are very different, and those factors contributed mightily to the spread and shape of urbanization in each place, and to the contours of the American and China Dreams. The American Dream conjures up visions of rugged individualistic cowboys taming the West, with help from immigrant Chinese building the railroads, and a massive influx of immigrants, most headed to big cities, entering through Ellis Island under the gaze of the Statue of Liberty. Both wide-open spaces and crowded tenements, peopled by folk free to do as they chose, fueled the American Dream.

China's strong central control, especially after the 1949 revolution, meant that the government largely decided what people could do, often with difficult consequences such as the Cultural Revolution. Government policy later decreed the forced movement off the farm, but it wasn't until the opening of the country to the world in the 1970s that effective and beneficial urbanization could begin.

What has been the impact of this accelerated, though delayed, move from farm to city? While it shares a lot superficially with the U.S.'s growth, it reflects another particular aspect of the China Dream. Both great transformations centered around the family. In the U.S., family farms slowly gave way to agribusiness, and farm children could learn other trades at universities. The Great Migration saw six million African Americans leave the rural South for northern cities between 1920 and 1970. Fed by the new technology, the new heartland of the American Dream, cities and their suburbs, swelled.

Fast-forward, literally, to China. To hit the 65 percent urbanization goal by 2025, still well below the Western average of 80 percent, will mean a massive program of infrastructure spending on everything from roads to houses to office buildings to high-speed trains to broadband towers and cables to pretty much everything. It's like a century of development all at once.

A CICC report called "New Infrastructure in China: New Drivers for Economic Growth and Potential Investment Opportunities," is worth a close look.[1] I've added some thoughts throughout.

According to the report:

"New infrastructures in China can be defined as support for new urban development, including energy conservation, environmental protection, advanced rail transit, and ultra-high-voltage and other forms of power transmission and distribution. Facilities for strategic emerging hi-tech sectors, including new materials, artificial intelligence, alternative energies, electric cars, new-generation information technologies (e.g., 5G, big data, Internet and Internet of Things), and advanced equipment such as robots and high-end computerized numerical-control (CNC) machine tools can be included in a broad sense."

There are amazing opportunities for investment here. It's one of the most exciting aspects of the China Dream because it affects so many people and, as plans turn into reality, creates so many changes in daily life. Back to CICC:

"The Chinese government highlighted the importance of investment and the potential demand for investment in its 2019 economic plans formulated at the Central Economic Work Conference. According to these plans, China is to upgrade technologies and equipment in manufacturing industries, accelerate commercialization of 5G technologies, and invest in new infrastructures such as artificial intelligence (AI), industrial internet, and the internet of things (IoT). Meanwhile, China also plans to invest more in intercity transit systems, logistic networks, and municipal infrastructures."

As I mentioned previously, it's always a good idea to pay close attention to government plans. They tend to get implemented. U.S. administrations' budgets may be stalled in Congress, but China's plans are always very much alive. CICC again:

"By thoroughly examining patterns of recent project approval, implementation, and sources and uses of the government's FAI-related funds . . . we may see higher investment growth in urban rail transit systems, poverty alleviation and rural infrastructure, telecom facilities, environmental protection, water and waste treatment systems, sports and cultural facilities, health care facilities, as well as low-income housing."

Let's break this down for a minute. Whether you think cities are good, believe in suburbs or exurbs, or revere the idyllic (and totally outdated) image of the farmer chugging along a newly plowed field on his tractor, cities are where the action is all over the world. And in China, as elsewhere, what it takes to build, grow, and maintain a city and connect it to other cities and towns and keep it safe and employ its residents and keep them healthy and happy, well, that's the whole strategy of economic development.

It's both an onion and a mushroom. The many layers of development fit tightly to each other. As it happens, urban development spreads and spreads. Infrastructure connects it all. And it's where the money flows.

Back to the CICC report:

"Geographically, we have observed higher growth of project pipelines for high-speed railway (HSR) investment in western China, as well as urban rail transit systems in eastern China. Infrastructure investment also receives a boost from accelerating the development of economic zones (EZ), such as the Beijing-Tianjin-Hebei EZ, the Yangtze River EZ, the Guangdong-Hong Kong-Macau Greater Bay Area, and regions covered by the Belt and Road Initiative."

XIONG'AN NEW AREA: A CASE STUDY

My KraneShares colleague Brendan Ahern traveled to one of the new megacities in 2017[2] and I've described his journey as follows. It sums up so much of what is happening with China's urbanization.

A three-hour drive from the Central Business District brings you to an area that most Beijing natives would have historically never had reason to visit.

China's next megacity, the Xiong'an New Area, was announced by the Chinese government on April 1, 2017.[3] Xiong'an is located about 170 km (106 miles) southwest of Beijing by car. The area is being built to help stimulate economic growth in Northern China and combat overcrowding in Beijing.[4] It consists of mostly agricultural land today but is expected to become a city covering more than 2,000 square kilometers.[5] To put this in perspective, that's almost three times the geographic size of New York City.[6]

Anyone visiting this new area might be reminded of a speech given by President Barack Obama at a joint press conference with China's President, Xi Jinping, in 2015. In the speech, he remarked that China's success in lifting hundreds of millions of people out of poverty has been "one of the most remarkable achievements in human history . . ."[7]

The results of China's success are the hundreds of apartment buildings lining the highway. These buildings are a testament to the positive effect that urbanization has had on China's people and economy. Over the past thirty years, the number of Chinese people living in urban areas has increased from 22.9 percent to 56.8 percent of its current 1.3 billion citizens.[8] The World Bank estimates that around one billion Chinese people, or 70 percent of its population, will be living in cities by 2030.[9]

One primary reason for this movement of people into cities is that living in urban areas in China generally allows for a much greater standard of living. The graph below reflects the difference in quality of life between urban and rural areas, showing how the annual disposable income of urban households greatly exceeds that of rural households. Additionally, urban areas in China, on average, have greater access to electricity, running water, sanitation facilities, health care, and higher education.

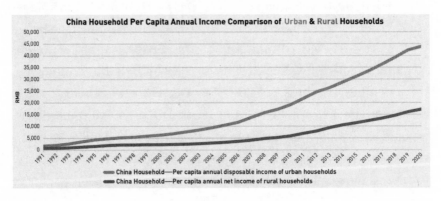

China Household Per Capita Annual Income Comparison of Urban & Rural Households

China Household—Per capita annual disposable income of urban households
China Household—Per capita annual net income of rural households

Data from Bloomberg as of 12/31/2020.

While the Xiong'an New Area is still largely just rural fields, it has the potential to become a metropolis on the scale of other global economic urban center powerhouses.

After all, this is not the first time China has planned and successfully constructed a megacity. Shenzhen and Shanghai's Pudong District were just small villages in the 1980s, but following their development by the Chinese government, they have grown to become some of the world's largest economic centers and currently have more than 10 million people in each city.

In the decade following Shenzhen's development by the government, its GDP grew at an annual rate of 40 percent until it reached $284 billion in 2016, greater than that of Portugal, Finland, and Vietnam.[10] Shenzhen is also home to the world's eighth largest stock exchange with a market capitalization of about $3 trillion. Shanghai had an even larger GDP than Shenzhen in 2016 at about $400 billion, and the Shanghai Stock Exchange is now the fourth largest stock market in the world with a market capitalization of over $4.5 trillion.

If Shenzhen and Shanghai Pudong were able to grow from villages to global economic centers in just twenty to thirty years, then the future of the Xiong'an New Area looks promising, and based on all of the real estate developers, cement trucks, and construction equipment visiting almost daily, it looks like companies in China feel the same way.

The Chinese government expects that its cities will continue to grow and urbanize, and while the Xiong'an New Area may seem to be in the middle of nowhere now, it will not remain that way for long.

The construction of this new megacity has significantly benefited investors in the Xiong'an New Area. Directly following the announcement on April 1, 2017, stocks of both national and regional cement companies soared. For example, Jidong Cement and BBMG Corp., two cement companies operating in the area, saw their stock prices grow by 69 percent and 95 percent respectively over the following two weeks.

Similarly, the value of real estate in the area skyrocketed. Housing prices more than tripled overnight, and real estate development companies saw the value of their stocks jump upward. China Fortune Land and RiseSun Real Estate are two such real estate companies that saw over 45 percent stock price growth across the same time period.

Overall, about forty companies related to the Xiong'an New Area had their stocks jump to the upper limit for daily gains on mainland China stock markets, and many continued to grow in the following weeks.

While the Xiong'an announcement spurred many Chinese companies to have sudden and explosive growth, the initial fervor to invest in the area will likely temper as the project takes shape over the next decade (the exact timeline has yet to be announced). The ultimate success of the project will require sustained attention and financial support from the central government and the relaxation of domestic migratory policies, which restrict some rural residents from leaving the countryside.

Ultimately, China's demographics make me optimistic about Xiong'an's success. Recall that the World Bank predicts one billion people will live in China's cities by 2030. With 780 million people in these cities today, this number must grow by more than 200 million between now and 2030 to meet the World Bank's predictions. This leads us to believe that China will need many more megacities in addition to Xiong'an over the next ten to twenty years.

If Xiong'an and other planned cities follow the trend of their predecessors, each reaching a size of about ten million people, then we believe China could need as many as twenty more megacities to sustain its rate of urbanization. The effect that twenty megacities might have on the Chinese mainland equity markets could be massive, and hundreds of regional and national companies could potentially see growth as a result.

Xiong'an highlights both the speed and significance of urbanization in China. It's a trend that's real and unstoppable.

A 2013 news report from *60 Minutes* titled "China's Real Estate Bubble"[11] featured footage of Zhengzhou city, full of brand-new condominiums, shopping malls, and offices all left mostly unoccupied. The primary flaw in the *60 Minutes* report is that Zhengzhou was represented as an entirely brand-new and unoccupied city. In fact, Zhengzhou is a major metropolitan area with over nine million people, about the same size as the Chicago metropolitan area.[12] The new district featured in the report is an annex to Zhengzhou and is only a small section of the city that was destined for expansion.

Since 2013, when the *60 Minutes* report aired, Zhengzhou's economy has boomed. It has grown to be China's number two special economic zone (an area designated by the government that is allowed to operate with more free market policies), with combined imports and exports reaching $7 billion in 2015. Zhengzhou is also now the world's largest site for smartphone production, with 80 percent of all iPhones manufactured there. The new city annex was built in Zhengzhou because rapid urbanization demanded more apartment buildings, and the supposed "Ghost City" was quickly absorbed by people moving to Zhengzhou and became fully occupied.

Stephen Roach, former Morgan Stanley chief economist and senior fellow at Yale University's Jackson Institute for Global Affairs, once said that China's modernization is "the greatest urbanization story the world has ever seen" and that ghost cities will soon become "thriving metropolitan areas."[13]

Ghost cities' prevalence in China, touted not just by *60 Minutes* but also by the *Wall Street Journal*, the BBC, and others, are grossly overstated and misleading. Even worse, they distract from the single most important trend in China over the past thirty-five years: the massive migration from rural areas to cities. As we've seen, in 1980, only 20 percent of China's population lived in cities, while today that figure is over 60 percent. China has 251 metropolitan areas with a population over two million, which is eight times the number of similar-sized metropolitan areas in the United States. China's per capita gross domestic product (GDP) has risen in tandem with increased urbanization, as more of its population gains access to education, higher wages, proper housing, running water, and reliable electricity. We're already starting to see that serving all of these new urban dwellers and giving them the standard of living they dream of will require investment, determination, imagination, and innovation on a scale greater than or equal to this mass migration.

TRANSPORTATION AND INFRASTRUCTURE

The China Dream has already seen vast movements of people from farm to city, and that will continue. But to allow all these people to stay connected with each other, as well as to pursue opportunity wherever it arises, vast investments in infrastructure are being made. Much like the U.S. Interstate Highway System and air travel enabled the American Dream, so will infrastructure investment fuel the China Dream. Actually, it's something the Chinese have long been good at.

I have visited the Great Wall many times, and I'm always amazed by its vastness and beauty. China has in recent decades figured out how to make it one of the world's most-visited tourist attractions while preserving and rebuilding it where necessary.

But at its heart, the Great Wall is one of history's greatest infrastructure projects. It provided a safe pathway along the then-border while also acting as an often-imperfect barrier to invasion.

The Wall often reminds me that China has been building infrastructure for a long time—think the Silk Road as well—and is currently doing so at an incredible pace.

Let's start with high-speed trains, truly a modern infrastructure marvel. Every weekday, in Beijing and Shanghai and Shenzhen and dozens of other Chinese cities, tens of thousands of commuters rush through soaring new terminals and hop on trains that take them back and forth to work.

Nothing special here, although unlike their fellow commuters in New York or Chicago, they can live up to two hundred miles from the office and still have only an hour or so commute. Intercity trains in China can travel about 350 miles per hour and have given millions of people the chance to work in Beijing or Shanghai despite living in much less expensive distant cities or towns.

China has built an astonishing 22,000 miles of high-speed rail tracks in the past decade or so, nearly ten times as much as Japan, which has the second most. The sleek trains that glide on these tracks are all made in China.

The Paulson Institute's MacroPolo group did an analysis in early 2021 that offers a good overview.[14]

"More than a decade since China began to link the country by high-speed rail (HSR), that network today stretches more than 22,000 miles and connects roughly 80% of Chinese cities. Each day, nearly 1,000 trains fan out from China's largest cities carrying six million people, or four times higher than the daily volume of air travel. And Beijing is not done yet: it intends to add another 6,000 miles of HSR by 2025 . . .

"Based on a careful cost-and-benefit analysis and using a framework similar to the World Bank's, we estimate that the HSR network confers a net benefit of $378 billion to the Chinese economy and has an annual ROI of 6.5."

And it doesn't stop at trains. The world's biggest and someday its busiest airport opened just outside Beijing in late 2019.

Beijing Daxing International Airport (PKX) cost more than $17 billion to build and has all the energy efficiency and passenger convenience one can imagine. The seven-hundred-thousand-square-meter terminal looks like a giant starfish from above, and will eventually see 100 million passengers a year, none of whom should have to walk more than eight minutes from security check-in to gate. The idea is to relieve congestion at Beijing's current airport, which itself handles about 100 million passengers a year.

And China plans to build more than two hundred new airports around the country in the next fifteen years for a total of 450 by 2035. Based on their track record, I'm sure they will.

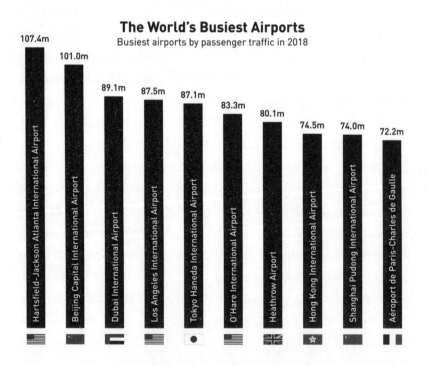

The World's Busiest Airports
Busiest airports by passenger traffic in 2018

- 107.4m — Hartsfield-Jackson Atlanta International Airport
- 101.0m — Beijing Capital International Airport
- 89.1m — Dubai International Airport
- 87.5m — Los Angeles International Airport
- 87.1m — Tokyo Haneda International Airport
- 83.3m — O'Hare International Airport
- 80.1m — Heathrow Airport
- 74.5m — Hong Kong International Airport
- 74.0m — Shanghai Pudong International Airport
- 72.2m — Aéroport de Paris-Charles de Gaulle

Data from Airport Council International and Statista.

Trains and planes are great, but people love cars. China now has more than 100,000 miles of expressways and 260,000 miles of highways, with enough cars, many of them now electric with more to come, to fill Beijing's seven ring roads at all times of the day.

Vital to transportation, of course, is the infrastructure—airports, railroads, roads, bridges—that allows planes, trains, and automobiles to function.

CICC reports that, for example, the government is constructing 535 miles of new or improved subway lines in cities, including Shanghai, Chongqing, and Jinan, at a cost of more than $100 billion. Even this massive expansion—nearly double the length of the New York City subway system—won't be enough. Systems currently serving 37 cities in China range from 420 miles in Shanghai and 415 miles in Beijing to 16 miles in Jinan. Nearly all of them have been expanded within the last five years.

All this spending is evident in subways like that in Beijing. The stations are vast and, in some cases, seem more like an airport than a subway station. Commuters tap or point their phones for entry and wait behind barriers for the silent and frequent trains.

As is evident from any map, most of China's people live in vast megacities on the East Coast. Since that's where the people are, that's where most of the infrastructure has been built. According to CICC, if we only consider China's level of infrastructure development east of the "Hu Line"—an imaginary line named after its creator that cuts across the country diagonally to divide it into two roughly equal areas— China's transport infrastructure density is comparable to that of developed countries.

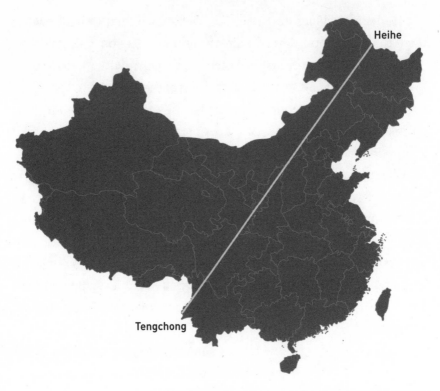

Only 4 percent of the population lives in the 64 percent of the country's land area west of the Hu Line, also known as the Heihe-Tengchong Line. Source: CICC Research.

According to the National Bureau of Statistics, China has about 4.77 million kilometers of roads, placing it third in the world—behind the U.S. (6.65 million kilometers) and India (5.6 million kilometers).

Urban rail transit accounts for only 15 percent of China's public transport system. This ratio is just 40 to 50 percent in large Chinese cities (e.g., Beijing and Shanghai), well below the average level (80 percent) in large overseas cities. Overseas data shows that the urban rail transit market begins growing explosively when the urbanization rate reaches

60 percent. CICC expects China's urban rail transit market to grow 10 to 15 percent annually over the next ten to fifteen years.

All of this infrastructure building is, of course, economically self-reinforcing, and is a key enabler of the China Dream. As cities grow, they require new ring roads and bus routes and subways and high-speed trains and highways and airports to connect it all. It's a huge economic stimulus as it all gets built, and it's a continuing economic stimulus as it allows billions of people to live out their dreams.

REAL ESTATE AND DEBT

As we discussed previously, China has gone to great lengths to improve its use of debt, and those efforts have seen results. However, one of the most difficult areas in which to instill market discipline is the real estate sector. A good example is the recent events with Evergrande.

As economic growth and the transformation from a manufacturing- and export-dependent economic model have happened at a rapid pace, so, too, has real estate development. Much of that expansion has been funded with debt, as happens all around the world. The question that China faces more than other more established modern economies is how to manage this debt without sacrificing future growth.

Leverage and real estate development come hand in hand in any developed market. In fact, one of the true signs of a developed market is the ability to fund the construction of homes, office buildings, shopping malls, and spaces that generally promote the welfare of the public through the use of leverage. Therefore, China's challenge in this arena may be significant but is by no means uncommon or unheard of.

China's issue here basically stems from two main factors: inflated prices and a tightly regulated property market.

Price inflation affects debt markets when real estate developers overstate the value at which they will be able to sell the properties that they develop. This is understandable given the intense growth China has seen and the tendency toward being optimistic about growth in the future. Price inflation cannot be solved in one fell swoop by some law or public program.

China is also getting help in curtailing real estate leverage. Moody's and S&P Global will apply their long-earned expertise in evaluating credit flows in the economy, especially to real estate developers, and will also be doing so from an objective perspective. Aiding in this effort as well are the many foreign financial institutions, such as investment banks Morgan Stanley and JPMorgan, which are both rapidly setting up shop in China without having to establish joint ventures with Chinese firms.

The property market in China is unlike that in the United States, not only due to local customs around living, such as the customary rule that a man must own a home before getting married, but also due to regulations, most notably those stemming from the Hukou system. The Hukou system is essentially an internal immigration regime. Moving between provinces or even cities currently requires approval from government authorities.

Unlike in America where one can pick up and move from New Jersey to New Mexico without notifying or receiving approval from anyone, Chinese citizens must go through immigration channels to move from Anhui province to Beijing or anywhere else. This system sounds strict. However, historically, vast developmental and economic differences between regions have convinced the central government that movement between them must be restricted to prevent overcrowding in major cities and the desertion of rural areas.

The Hukou system also has a bearing on real estate. Naturally, one must be permitted to live in Beijing before buying or renting a home in the city. Therefore, many potential customers are left out of the property market and, as a result, prices for real estate assets can be kept at reasonable levels.

Admittedly, the Hukou system is not likely to be done away with any time soon. Think overcrowding in Beijing is bad now? Just wait until any resident of a rural province is legally permitted to move there. However, the system is likely to be updated as China's market undergoes further reforms.

SMART CITIES

As the cities expand, the race is on to use technology to make them "smart."

Given the increasing urbanization, it's logical that China has become a leader in developing smart cities, with all new buildings incorporating the latest technology in Wi-Fi and communications and security and many older buildings being retrofitted.

CICC has studied smart cities in depth, and a recent report points out non-obvious consequences of these developments that both explain China a little better and foreshadow issues we're going to have to address eventually in the U.S. Here's a summary of their report.

Since its coining by IBM in 2008, the concept of the "smart city" has been adopted by many governments. Its definition isn't really fixed. Loosely, it's about combining digital technology with city management. China's *Economic Daily* once described a smart city as being supported by a new generation of information technologies (such as internet, IoT, cloud computing, remote sensing, global positioning systems, and geographic information systems) that enable it to intelligently perceive, respond and adapt, and develop in a sustainable way.

Smart cities are going to need massive new infrastructure, security and surveillance facilities, construction of sensors for the industrial internet, and support from data centers, the providers of which all should see huge growth and are worth considering as investments. China needs to, and will, given priorities in the latest Five-Year Plan, continue to improve data sharing and collection facilities, which means large-scale construction and demand.

Smart cities require municipalities to combine digital technology with city management. The December 2018 Central Economic Work Conference, which laid out city plans, among other things, stressed that China would step up efforts to build and invest in new infrastructure such as artificial intelligence (AI), Internet of Things (IoT), data centers, and the industrial internet. This means smart cities will actually happen.

This will lead to strong demand for security and surveillance facilities as well as for the industrial internet. Chinese researchers are already making breakthroughs in AI technology that will reshape the video surveillance industry. The development of the industrial internet will bring opportunities for equipment suppliers, software and service providers, communications companies, and the manufacturing industry, including Alibaba Cloud, Tencent Cloud, Huawei Cloud, Ecloud, and Unicloud.

According to MarketsandMarkets.com, the global smart city market will reach $820.7 billion in 2025 from $410.8 billion in 2020, a CAGR (compound annual growth rate) of 14.8 percent.[15] It could grow even more as China continues to improve its smart cities and upgrade infrastructure such as security and surveillance facilities, the industrial internet, and internet data centers (IDCs).

Already, there are video cameras in use all over China. The market is growing by more than $20 billion a year and will grow even faster as breakthroughs in AI technology come online. AI technology will also boost the growth of China's manufacturing industry, given that industrial data is massive and complicated, and the scale of China's manufacturing industry is larger than in almost all other countries. The key to this is a technology called industrial sensors, little gizmos that provide constant updates on how machines and their processes are working, often so that they can be tuned for the best output. Industrial sensors are the main infrastructure in the digital manufacturing stage, and industrial communications and the industrial "cloud," or shared computing power, are the main infrastructure in networked manufacturing, the next big thing.

To keep track of all this data for smart cities, there will need to be more industrial data centers, huge computer farms shared by many companies all over the country. The China Academy of Information and Communications (CAICT) estimates the country's IDC market will grow 32 percent each year for the foreseeable future. There is also going to be considerable growth in so-called edge data centers, near their specific users, which tend to save energy.

This sort of thing is good news because surging urban populations have caused environmental, employment, housing, transport, and safety challenges, and new technologies are needed to support city development.

Despite much progress, China still needs to promote innovation and make breakthroughs in smart cities. It needs to solve problems like the prevalence of data silos, isolated city management systems, similar networks in different cities, inefficient construction, and, though unusual, a lack of a long-term plan. The construction of smart cities remains in the initial stages, while a lot of existing urban buildings remain traditional, that is, not very high tech.

It's not just smart cities that are driving innovations in research. Companies all over China are doing breakthrough work in virtually all areas of daily life. In the next chapter we'll look at another aspect of the China Dream that excites me—trends in services and technology.

CHAPTER NINE
Trends in Services and Technology

As mentioned earlier, China's new growth agenda focuses on services, most of them involving data and telecommunications technologies, artificial intelligence, and the so-called Internet of Things, the networking of many appliances and systems to allow them to exchange data.

CICC sees thirteen major trends, many of them surprising, listed here with my own comments and explanations. There is much to digest here, but I hope you'll benefit from it. I have gotten a lot of investing ideas out of these trends, and I hope you will, too.

TREND NO.1: EDUCATION AND ENTERTAINMENT BECOME MORE INTERTWINED

Fifth Generation (5G) telecom technology will make education and entertainment more intertwined. That's because 5G will free up workers from labor-intensive industries and more people would turn to education content creation and service industries. In addition, big data and artificial intelligence will enable content customization, so that educational content can be tailored to individuals, as can entertainment content. New technologies such as virtual reality (VR) and augmented reality (AR) will change the way people acquire content and provide new educational and entertainment experiences, including gaming and exercise programs. These technologies would also change the role of teachers from simply imparting teaching knowledge to helping students make and adjust learning plans and ensuring they complete the plans.

TREND NO.2: PERSONALIZED SERVICES REPLACE STANDARDIZED SERVICES

As massive data helps depict the behavior of individuals more accurately, personalized or customized services will replace standardized services, reshaping many industries.

Importantly, 5G will reduce the cost of customized services as massive data more accurately depicts the behavior of individuals. These services will also reduce the demand for human labor. The replacement of standardized consumer services by personalized or customized services would refocus health care services from medical treatment to health intervention. Insurance services are likely to be fully customized based on big data. Private banking services are likely to be accessible to all consumers because data analysis would make them cheaper to administer.

TREND NO.3: POPULATION AGING IS NO LONGER AN ISSUE

5G network-based AI or robots will be able to replace humans in most production and service industries, freeing up more workers to expand the health and services industries, as well as claim more leisure time for themselves. This is critical to serve China's aging population.

In large part because of the now-abandoned one child per family regulations, the number of children per family in China has declined. The census released in May, 2021 showed a 15% drop in births in 2020 from the year before. Over the past fifty years, the proportion of Chinese children under the age of fourteen has fallen from 41 percent to 17 percent, while the proportion of those over the age of sixty-five has grown from 4 percent to 12 percent. This trend may slowly reverse, as the government is now encouraging larger families and opening in vitro fertility clinics.

But with people born from 1962–1970 about to retire in the next five to ten years, 5G and AI technology will come online to increase the productivity of the smaller workforce. Health-care and housing companies catering to the elderly in China will benefit from this new boom.

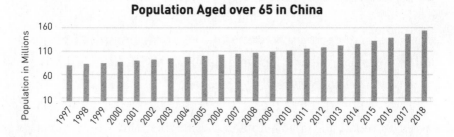

Population Aged over 65 in China

TREND NO.4: THE ERA OF MASS-PRODUCED STANDARDIZED PRODUCTS ENDS AND BUSINESS MODEL INNOVATION BECOMES MORE IMPORTANT

As technology gaps narrow, innovations in design and unique services will be key. With advances in technology shrinking the differences in products and services, internet innovation will be increasingly focused on business models, such as new ways to attract revenue through sub-scriptions, and services such as ride hailing and shopping. The broad-based application of 5G technologies will create new possibilities in both of these areas. Telecom companies providing high-quality services on a large scale will further move into business and personal life in the 5G era, as high-quality services need to be customized according to the actual needs of users. This means these telecommunications companies will continue to absorb, or be absorbed by, entertainment, consumer prod-uct, and other non-telecom companies.

TREND NO.5: INDUSTRIAL WORKERS ARE REPLACED

Intelligent and automated production will free workers from labor-intensive industries. More people would work in innovative service industries. The Internet of Things will provide data and management support to automated production, of vital importance to the develop-ment of intelligent manufacturing and smart agriculture. This in turn will provide much cheaper food and manufactured products while trim-ming waste and energy use.

The 5G network would promote fast upgrade of technologies related to remote operation and automated manufacturing, allowing large manufacturers to achieve more intelligent manufacturing and require fewer workers on production lines.

TREND NO.6: FEWER POLICE OFFICERS ARE NEEDED

Cities would become "smarter," ideally reducing crime rates and acci-dent rates and making public services more intelligent and convenient.

As an integral part of traditional city management, police organi-zations, due to the nature of their services, are human-intensive. Smart cities in the 5G era will have a more intelligent city management ecosystem and less city management needs. The management function would be changed into the planning function, making public services more intelligent and convenient. The Chinese, too, have to stand in long lines at their equivalent of the Department of Motor Vehicles to get licenses renewed. Smart city technology should eliminate those DMV lines.

TREND NO.7: IMPROVED FORECASTING OF NATURAL DISASTERS WILL REDUCE THEIR DAMAGE

With the Internet of Things and artificial intelligence technologies, we will be able to digitize the real world and improve forecasting and monitoring in meteorology, geology, and ecology. It is still difficult to predict natural disasters at present, and many natural disasters have caused great losses of life and property. The ability to predict natural disasters depends on how much we know about nature. However, our knowledge about nature has been limited by data availability.

In the 5G era, we would be able to collect much more data on the natural environment leveraging the IoT. Scientists may make new breakthroughs in meteorology, hydrology, geology, and ecology with the help of big data. Our ability to monitor and manage the environment is likely to be significantly enhanced and losses from natural disasters are likely to be reduced.

TREND NO.8: GOVERNMENT BECOMES THE LARGEST BUYER OF DATA SERVICES

In the 5G era, government outsourcing to companies of data collection, processing and analysis that is currently done by some governments will accelerate. The government would be responsible for policymaking and become smaller. AI, automation, and information technology will free the government from its routine management and service duties to focus more on policymaking and implementation. As the government is freed up from social management duties to focus more on data analysis and policymaking, it would reduce related personnel, just like an agricultural or industrial firm.

TREND NO.9: NETWORKS BECOME DECENTRALIZED

The current internet is built around people as end users in networks. Customers must buy what is offered. It has a centralized structure, with key users and companies with large user bases. As the amount of information on the Internet of Things, from linked devices in the home and office, grows exponentially, networks will become more personalized, with future services customized. Artificial Intelligence will process this information and the IoT in the 5G era will need intermediary companies to process all this new information and tailor services to customers. This is where to look for growth, from personal grooming to ride-sharing to dining and movie choices. Future, decentralized networks will favor smaller, innovative companies offering services demanded by consumers over legacy companies that rely on large traffic on centralized platforms as their main competitive advantage. In a 5G world that advantage vanishes.

TREND NO.10: ZHONGGUANCUN-TYPE FIRMS REPLACE SILICON VALLEY–TYPE ONES AS GLOBAL INNOVATION CENTERS

The key to the Internet of Things' benefits lies in the size of networks—that is, the number of users, the amount of IoT connections, and the total traffic volume. Data would be the basis for sustainable innovation of products and services. Here's where China has a real edge. Zhongguancun-type companies, meaning those high-tech firms based in Beijing's innovation hub district, are taking the lead in global business model innovation, leveraging their vast networks. These companies are Silicon Valley-type firms on steroids. They are the biggest and fastest-growing tech companies in the world. The world's largest 5G network they are building will attract research and innovation institutions and talent and trigger new waves of entrepreneurship with the largest population, the most IoT connections, and the most active business model innovation.

Speed is of the essence in technological innovation and service, and that's what 5G offers. The global average network connection speed has risen three-and-a-half times from 3G to 4G, and the speed increase is even larger in China. Network penetration and speed in China have both increased significantly thanks to the government's policies to increase speed and cut price. China has one of the fastest network speeds among the world's major populous nations.

As network infrastructure expands, the quality of mobile networks has improved quickly, and faster network speed has paved the way for innovation of internet services. At the same time, more users have chosen to access the internet through mobile phones as data charges drops. The mobile internet has been used more frequently and the time spent on it has also increased significantly.

For example, 5G will make it even easier to order goods and services such as ride-sharing services or paying bills, while also helping providers reach more far-flung subscribers.

China's massive IoT connections help carriers penetrate the IoT and vertical industries. The low latency and high reliability of carriers' networks are paving the way for their expansion in the industrial internet, which we've seen is the key to smart cities.

China's 5G technology R&D is at the forefront globally. Equipment vendors such as Huawei and ZTE, as well as three major carriers, have conducted in-depth cooperation in 5G technology. They have completed first and second phases of 5G technology R&D testing and NSA (non-stand-alone) testing in the third phase. At present, the third-stage SA (stand-alone) testing is fully underway. The three major carriers in China all started pre- commercial use in 2019 and commercial use in 2020. Initially, 5G will likely be launched primarily in densely populated urban areas and industrial innovation areas, in order to test 5G network performance and usage before deployment in suburban and rural areas.

Legacy 3G development was largely controlled by European companies like Nokia and Ericsson. The United States controlled 4G development, and companies like AT&T, Verizon, Google, Facebook, and others thrived. But now 5G will be led by China, and companies like China Telecom, Huawei, Alibaba, Tencent, and Baidu will become global leaders. As we saw in chapter six, the Belt and Road Initiative will also be a platform for China to expand 5G across the 120 countries that have signed up. Today, Germany and Italy have already committed to China 5G and are currently working with Huawei to build out the infrastructure. Indeed, 5G is one of the key pillars for China's globalization.

China's desire to increase domestic consumption led Premier Li Keqiang to announce the Internet Plus strategy at the 2015 National People's Congress. The new policy drove economic growth by integrating internet technologies with traditional sectors and focus on fostering new industries and business development, including ecommerce, industrial internet, and internet finance. Premier Li's plan helped supercharge three trends in the global internet sector in which China is increasingly becoming a world leader: the use of mobile phones, online to offline commerce, and cloud computing.

TREND NO. 11: MOBILE PHONE USAGE
CONTINUES TO INCREASE

The adoption and use of mobile phones is a leading trend among consumers around the world. In 2014, the number of worldwide mobile users was 5.6 billion and rose to 6.6 billion by the end of 2020. China represents a significant share of this population with more than 10.7 percent of all mobile users worldwide. The rise of high-quality, low-cost cell phone manufacturers has made cell phone use nearly ubiquitous in China's major cities. A variety of applications and services have emerged to compete for the attention of China's mobile audience. One such application is WeChat, which has more than one billion users. WeChat is owned by Tencent, a Chinese technology company focused on providing internet and mobile services, and combines the functions of an online messaging system with those of a social media platform.

Mobile-cellular telephone subscriptions			
	2000	2019	Growth multiple
India	3,577,095	1,151,480,361	322x
Russia	3,263,200	239,795,946	73x
China	85,260,000	1,725,695,000	20x
South Africa	8,339,000	96,972,459	12x
Brazil	23,188,171	207,046,813	9x
Argentina	6,487,950	58,606,442	9x
Malaysia	5,121,748	44,601,400	9x
Poland	6,747,000	52,268,128	8x
South Korea	26,816,398	68,892,541	3x

Source: International Telecommunications Union
statistics database as of 12/31/2019.

TREND NO. 12: ONLINE TO OFFLINE COMMERCE (O2O) INCREASES

While O2O commerce has existed for several years, it has recently become a vital aspect of the ecommerce business model. The term O2O originated in the United States but is more commonly used by Chinese ecommerce companies to explain the next step in the consumer experience. O2O commerce is the principle of connecting the online digital world to the offline world through the integration of internet-connected devices.

Baidu owns an O2O product called Baidu Waimai that delivers food to customers and is comparable to Seamless in the United States. For instance, a consumer in Beijing simply has to enter his address into Waimai and choose from a list of restaurants that will provide delivery service. This product benefits both the supply and demand side of the market by providing suppliers with a larger consumer base and giving consumers discount incentives from ordering online. Baidu has seen the gross merchandise value of its O2O products double each year. Meituan, which we'll look at later, is also a major player in food delivery, and other ecommerce giants such as Alibaba and Tencent are also investing in O2O development.

TREND NO. 13: CLOUD COMPUTING USAGE INCREASES

Mobile adoption and O2O commerce need a storage system capable of holding the vast amounts of new data created every day. Since the amount of data generated is increasing exponentially, old methods of storing information on a computer server in one physical location are outdated and cannot meet these requirements. The use of cloud computing now allows companies to store their data in online servers that have nearly unlimited capacity. Cloud computing benefits large companies because the stored data can be accessed and shared from anywhere, even international offices.

The 25 Largest Internet Companies in the World by Revenue		
Company Name	Last 12 Months Revenue ($ Billion)	Country
Amazon	386	USA
Netflix	250	USA
Google	182.5	USA
Rakuten	145.5	Japan
Wayfair	141.5	USA
JD.com	107.3178295	China
Baidu	107.1	China
Alibaba	99.87596899	China
Facebook	86	USA
Tencent	70.41860465	China
Suning.com	38.62015504	China
PayPal	21.5	USA
Salesforce	21.25	USA
Meituan	16.27906977	China
Adobe	12.9	USA
Uber	12.1	USA
NetEase	11.42635659	China
eBay	10.7	USA
Bloomberg	10.5	USA
Spotify	7.9	USA
Zalando	7.4	Germany
Booking.com	6.7	USA
Kuaishou	6.062015504	China
ByteDance	5.736434109	China
Expedia	5.2	USA

Source: Bloomberg as of 2/28/2020.

China's internet companies have adopted cloud computing because it provides a more practical and efficient way of storing data gathered from the country's 668 million internet users. For example, Alibaba, the largest retailer in China, owns a cloud computing service called Aliyun, which generates more than $60 million a quarter in revenue from selling storage services to consumers. Similarly, Tencent and Baidu have cloud products they are looking to expand both domestically and internationally.

In the next chapter, "Commerce and Ecommerce," we'll look at what's already happened in technology and commerce as it transforms Chinese life.

CHAPTER TEN
Commerce and Ecommerce

The China Dream is being fueled by constant innovation and lightning-fast adoption of new technologies. A lot of this centers on shopping, giving consumers more choice in what they buy, how they buy it, and how it gets to them. This is enabling perhaps the fastest and most inclusive increase in living standards the world has ever seen. It's at the heart of the China Dream for billions. Nowhere is it better seen than in phone and internet technology.

It's barely 9 AM on a sunny summer day outside the Fortune Financial Center in Beijing's central business district. But the half-dozen little electric vans are already lined up on the street outside the sixty-one-story office building, nestled among other brand-new behemoths in the city's burgeoning business district. Drivers for JD.com and other online marketplaces unload mounds of packages and express-mail envelopes, then hunch down and get busy on their phones. Soon there's a steady trickle of office workers from HSBC Holdings and other tenants of the skyscraper, who, summoned by text message, come down to pick up their packages.

A twentysomething woman in a black-and-white polka-dot dress picks up a box that might contain a new pair of shoes. Another in a floral dress picks up a flat envelope that looks like work. A young man in a blue shirt, blue jeans, and bright blue shoes points his phone at a QR code and gets three envelopes and a soft package. The average charge for each envelope is about eight U.S. cents. The scene will be repeated in the afternoon, and twice a day through the rest of the workweek.

It's a great convenience for the online sellers, the delivery companies, and the buyers. And it's another example of flexibility in overcoming hurdles. The delivery companies wouldn't mind delivering to offices, but they're not allowed inside the huge skyscrapers for security reasons. So the sidewalk distribution, possible in the age of the ubiquitous smartphone, sprang up.

Of course, no cash changes hands because, as we've seen, virtually nobody in big Chinese cities carries cash anymore. Kevin Liu of CICC says he used to carry around a big wad of bills and a pocketful of change, reducing that a bit with the advent of ATM machines and credit cards, but now he carries neither cash nor cards. He uses his phone to pay for everything.

Chinese dreamers also love to shop—and increasingly to shop for the world's best luxury goods. Take a stroll through any of the hundreds of high-end malls in hotels and office buildings in any big Chinese city. They seem to be clusters of shops from New York's Fifth Avenue, Paris's Champs-Élysées, Tokyo's Ginza, and Chicago's Magnificent Mile, all catering to wealthy shoppers in air-conditioned comfort. Prada. Louis Vuitton. FAO Schwarz. Gucci. Yves St. Laurent.

Why are all these luxury brands here? Because Chinese people buy one-third of the world's luxury goods. Think about that for a moment.

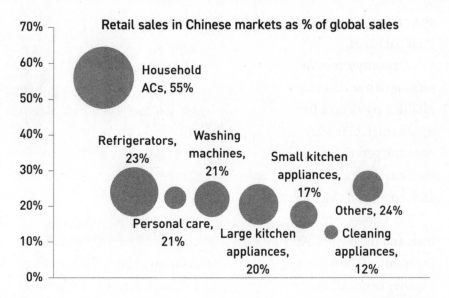

Source: CICC Research.

As we've seen, a big part of the China Dream is aspirational. Lower middle–class people want education and good jobs and better housing and a nice car for themselves and their families. Middle-class people may want to become upper class, and upper-class people may want to become millionaires. Along the way, as wealth flows, they mark their journeys by buying luxury goods that make them happy. The same thing happens in the U.S., Europe, and Japan. But as with most things that happen in China, the sheer scale is staggering.

The Chinese love their malls, but they also love a bargain at duty-free shops when they travel. Chinese purchases in overseas duty-free shops are four to five times as much as their spending in domestic ones.

As the following chart shows, the combination of ease of buying and a growing middle class eager to consume has contributed to a steady and healthy rise in retail sales.

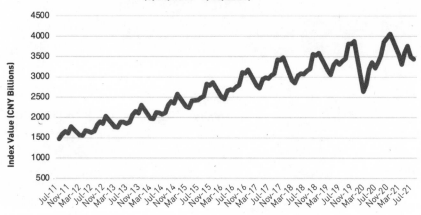

Value of Monthly China Retail Sales Index
(7/31/2011–9/30/2021)

Data from Bloomberg as of 09/30/2021.

And as the chart below shows, much of this spending is for high-end luxury goods.

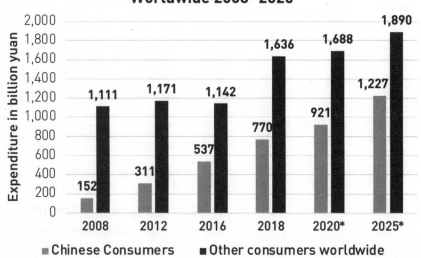

Spending on Luxury Items in China and Worldwide 2008–2025

■ Chinese Consumers   ■ Other consumers worldwide

Data from Statista, retrieved 12/31/2020. *Forecasts.

"Many investors are surprised to learn that China's retail sales surpassed that of the United States in 2019 when China clocked 5.8 trillion dollars' worth of goods sold versus 5.5 trillion dollars here in the United States. Even with the world's largest middle-class population, China still has immense potential for further consumption growth," my colleagues Brendan Ahern and Xiabing Su shared recently.[1] "Recent advancements in ecommerce platform technologies and discounted group buying programs have helped domestic brands expand their reach to lower-tier cities.

"We are also seeing how rising incomes in China have contributed to an overall consumption upgrade, consisting of a stronger preference for high-quality products, brand loyalty, and more luxury spending. New technology infrastructure, such as mobile payments, big data, artificial intelligence (AI), and cloud computing, is significantly enhancing the shopping experience, making it much more convenient and efficient as well as enabling companies to reach much larger audiences."

CHINA'S TOP LUXURY DRINKS

KraneShares' Xiabing Su has conducted extensive research on her home country's finest products. She shared her findings and her impressions with me as case studies of our strongest investments. She's one of our most valued researchers, and her report shows why. I've tasted or used most of these products and while some of it is not to Western taste, it all works for China.

"Kweichow Moutai has become one of the most prestigious and wanted gifts in China. Kweichow Moutai earns its name as the spirit of China because of its extraordinary taste. It is the only alcoholic beverage presented as an official gift by Chinese embassies in foreign countries. In 1972, Chinese premier Zhou Enlai used the liquor to entertain U.S.

President Richard Nixon during the state banquet for his presidential visit to China. In 1974, the U.S. Secretary of State Henry Kissinger told Deng Xiaoping, China's future leader, that 'I think if we drink enough Moutai, we can solve anything.'

"Kweichow Moutai has been a symbol of Chinese culture and also a display of status and wealth because of its limited supply. The price of Moutai stays at an all-time high. People also buy Moutai as a kind of investment, looking for an increase in value. Kweichow Moutai's company value has reached 402 billion dollars, followed by another Chinese liquor brand, Wuliangye, with a valuation of 176 billion dollars." [2]

At a five-star hotel restaurant, Xiabing Su was surprised not to see Moutai on their liquor shelf, so she asked the bartender where it was. She told her that Moutai was in short supply, despite its luxury cost. "The wholesale price is 1,499 yuan [~232 dollars], but now the retail price is over 4,000 yuan [~620 dollars]," she told her.

The report continues: "Many customers buy Moutai for collection, [or] they make appointments in advance." When Xiabing Su asked about Wuliangye, another popular luxury drink, the bartender told her that she had it in stock. "If you can't buy Moutai, the next best option is Wuliangye," she explained. "They are both good liquor brands in China, ranked number one and number two."

Kweichow Moutai and Wuliangye rank highest among liquor brands globally in terms of market cap. Combined, these two brands are worth more than the next six leading liquor brands collectively. Also, Kweichow Moutai ranks highest among beverage brands globally in terms of market cap, recently surpassing Coca-Cola in April 2021.

FOODS AND FLAVORS

Also according to Xiabing Su, "In terms of food culture as a part of a tradition, different flavors were created many generations ago and the recipes often remain as family secrets. Soy sauce and oyster sauce are two of the key flavors, and they have become an indispensable component when used for cooking Chinese dishes or simply as condiments. The global soy sauce market size is projected to reach $59.13 billion by 2025, increasing at a CAGR (compound annual growth rate) of 5.9 percent between 2019 and 2025, according to the KBV Research Global Soy Sauce Market Report. Haitian, the top brand of flavoring, is used by almost all Chinese families and restaurants.

"Haitian is also one of the essential suppliers for supermarkets, with around three hundred different product categories, including four-star products. The company has generated revenues of more than RMB 1 billion (~155 million dollars).

Shuanghui

Xiabing Su continues, "One of the most famous brands of sausage in China is Shuanghui. In 2013, Shuanghui bought Smithfield Foods, the largest U.S. pork processor, for 7.1 billion dollars. Apart from the taste, the meat of Shuanghui is also known for its quality and reliability. Even during the pandemic in the first half of 2020 in China, the revenue of Shuanghui reached 36 billion yuan (around 5 billion dollars), with an increase of 42 percent over the same period from the previous year."

Haier and Gree

Xiabing Su adds, "In terms of refrigerators and other electric appliances, which are used in everybody's home, Haier and Gree are the most universal choices because they have a strong reputation for quality and a large market share. China's home appliance market is posting the highest growth rate globally and is projected to reach more than $130 billion by the end of 2026. China's three largest appliance manufacturers—Midea Group, Gree Electric Appliances, and Haier Smart Home—account for roughly 80 percent of the combined value of China's top ten appliance manufacturers.

"Even so, these home appliance companies are still expanding their sales channels. Taking advantage of internet shopping and livestreaming, Dong Mingzhu, chairwoman of Gree Electric, also known as the mainland's 'home appliance queen,' started her own livestream to sell Gree products via different platforms like TikTok, JD, and Kuaishou. The cumulative sales of her five live broadcasts have exceeded 178 billion yuan (about 27 billion dollars)."

Li-Ning and Anta

Xiabing Su continues, "People are gradually shifting to Chinese domestic brands because they offer lower prices without compromising quality as they can work directly with local manufacturers."

I've seen this in many cases now where people are proud of the products being produced in China. Also, "Guochao," meaning fashion and design that incorporates Chinese cultural elements, has become extremely hot among Chinese young people. Two of the most popular "Guochao" brands are Li-Ning and Anta. Both of the companies started from sportswear, and they made innovations both internally and externally. In 2019, Anta achieved revenue of 34 billion yuan (about 5 billion dollars), a 30 percent increase from the previous year. In the first half of 2020, the revenue of China's Off-White, Li-Ning, reached 6 billion yuan (~942 million dollars), with a 21 percent increase in net profit.

According to Xiabing Su, "The purchasing power of China's population of 1.4 billion people is simply tremendous. We believe that that purchasing power provides a strong investment case for owning the companies whose products are being purchased by China's population."[3]

Every time I walk around a big city in China or talk to people there, the more true Xiabing's reporting above seems to me.

INTERNET AND DIGITAL PAYMENT

How do the people of China discover and purchase the millions of items they consume? As mentioned previously, internet use has surged in China like nowhere else.

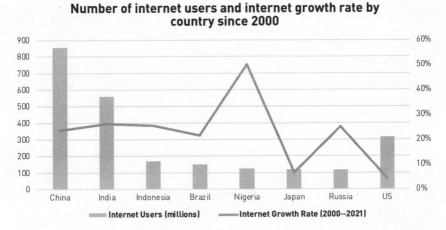

Number of internet users and internet growth rate by country since 2000

Internet Users (millions) — Internet Growth Rate (2000–2021)

Data from World Bank and Internet World Stats as of 12/31/2019.

China now far outstrips the U.S. in internet use and percentage of retail sales made online.

China / U.S. Internet Statistics	China	US
Total internet population	989mm[1]	299mm[2]
% of population with internet access	70.4%[1]	85.8%[2]
Country's share of world internet users	21.2%[2]	6.4%[2]
Ecommerce market size 2020	$1.8T[3]	$861B[4]
Total retail sales 2020	$6T[3]	$4T[4]
Online retail sales as % of total 2020	30%[3]	21%[4]

1. Data from Statista and the World Bank as of 2/9/2021. Retrieved 6/30/2021.
2. Data from Statista and the World Bank as of 1/27/2021. Retrieved 6/30/2021.
3. National Bureau of Statistics of China. Note: Figures converted from Chinese renminbi to USD as of 6/30/2021.
4. Digital Commerce 360. "US ecommerce grows 44.0% in 2020." January 29, 2021.

For a television show we were making, I bought a box of popcorn at The Place movie house in central Beijing using a cell phone. I pointed at the popcorn, the nice young lady behind the counter pointed her handheld device at my phone, and in a click or two I was enjoying my popcorn.

According to the *South China Morning Post*, merchants in various places are experimenting with facial software spearheaded by Ant Financial and Tencent that will ultimately replace the phones—smile into the camera and your payment is made. This development will likely help the elderly who might struggle to use their phones to pay.[4]

Two apps are leading the way: WeChat Pay by Tencent and Alipay by Alibaba, whose combined transaction volumes have already surpassed the legacy global payment duo Visa and Mastercard.

Alipay is ecommerce driven while WeChat Pay is driven by social media. The two dominate the payment market with a combined market share of 92 percent. Currently, Alipay controls 54 percent of the market

Top 10 Chinese Companies	Primary Business	China Internet Companies		Comparable U.S. Business	U.S. Internet Companies	
		1 Year Average Revenue Growth Rate	5 Year Average Revenue Growth Rate		1 Year Average Revenue Growth Rate	5 Year Average Revenue Growth Rate
TENCENT HOLDINGS LTD	Social Media	27%	38%	Facebook	19%	38%
MEITUAN-CLASS B	Online Delivery	17%	46%	GrubHub	31%	38%
PINDUODUO INC-ADR	Ecommerce	73%	729%	Groupon	-31%	-11%
ALIBABA GRP-ADR	Ecommerce	31%	47%	Amazon	31%	28%
JD.COM INC-ADR	Ecommerce	28%	34%	Amazon	31%	28%
BAIDU INC	Search	0%	12%	Google	11%	19%
JD HEALTH INTERN	Online Health Care	33%	40%	Teladoc Health	66%	68%
NETEASE INC-ADR	Gaming	20%	36%	Activision Blizzard	18%	12%
TAL EDUCATION GROUP-ADR	Online Education	25%	50%	Chegg	48%	15%
BILIBILI INC-ADR	Entertainment	72%	161%	Roku	55%	41%
		Average: 32%	Average: 119%		Average: 28%	Average: 28%

Source: Bloomberg as of 12/31/2020.

and WeChat Pay controls 38 percent. The slices have remained the same for a while, but the overall pie has expanded significantly. A customer purchases items at a café by scanning a QR code. Mobile payments also represent an inroad into the banking industry.

The use of mobile payment apps often means users keep money in mobile wallets operated by companies like Alibaba and Tencent. These companies are thereby able to offer basic banking services such as savings accounts and loans. The Chinese consumer is leapfrogging away from cash, credit cards, and the legacy banking system, which has proven very hard to do in the U.S. and Europe.

Top 10 Global Internet Companies By Market Cap	
Apple	$2.2T
Tencent	$2.2T
Amazon	$1.6T
Google	$1.2T
Facebook	$773.8B
Alibaba	$647.8B
Netflix	$231.2B
Salesforce	$203.5B
JD.com	$147.8B
Booking.com	$90.6B
Total	$9.3T

Data from Bloomberg as of 1/5/2021.

It took Apple until 2019 to roll out its own debit card, and many vendors in the U.S. are still acquiring the infrastructure needed to process mobile payments. Ant Financial, an affiliate of Alibaba, is a great example of the entrance of Chinese internet companies into banking. The company was formed as a separate entity after the massive success of Alibaba's mobile payments app, Alipay. The company operates Alipay and provides a wide variety of financial services such as accessible finance, savings accounts, and remittance services. The company also operates the world's largest money-market fund with $211 billion in assets.

Tencent's growth, especially in gaming, is expected to improve as newly launched games gather momentum and generate more revenue. Analysts continue to highlight the growth prospects of Tencent's businesses. Tencent Cloud is now China's second-largest cloud service provider and captures 11 percent of the market. Tencent Cloud is also pursuing an intense international push into the Japanese market, and more overseas expansions are planned for later this year.

Alibaba is a conglomerate primarily engaged in the ecommerce industry. The company operates an online marketplace offering a wide variety of consumer goods. The company has also branched out into new industries, including fintech, cloud computing, logistics, and entertainment.

Alibaba's growth is driven by two customer segments: the middle class in urban cities and customers in lower-tier cities and rural areas. Fast-moving consumer goods (FMCG), apparel, consumer electronics, and home furnishing categories drove the strong gross merchandise value (GMV) growth.

HISTORICALLY, ALIBABA HAS CONSISTENTLY OUTPERFORMED AMAZON IN TERMS OF PROFIT MARGINS.

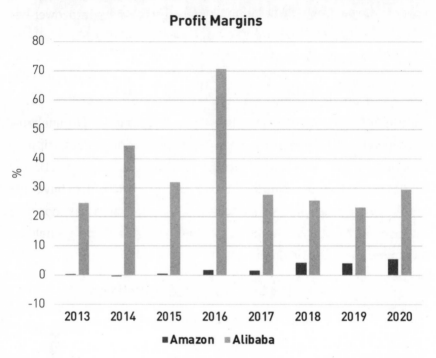

Profit Margins

Data from Bloomberg as of 12/31/2020.

There are two other companies worthy of note in this space. Baidu provides comprehensive web search services to Chinese consumers. The company is analogous to Google in the United States. Baidu has amassed an immense market share in China and is the country's most popular search engine. Similar to America's Google, Baidu is a nimble innovator with significant investments in both artificial intelligence research and autonomous vehicles.

JD.com is primarily involved in ecommerce. JD owns a large and growing marketplace for a wide variety of goods. Also, they have vertically integrated by offering their own logistics service. The majority of

JD.com's present customer base is mostly located in relatively well-off first- and second-tier cities and its penetration rate in these markets is fairly high. The company is therefore motivated to move into lower-tier cities and rural areas in China as well as areas outside China.

SINGLES' DAY: A CASE STUDY

Only in China could an unofficial holiday celebrating being single grow into the biggest ecommerce shopping day in the world, far outstripping Cyber Monday in the U.S. Started as an alternative to Valentine's Day by Chinese college students in 1993, the Singles' Day tradition to buy a gift for oneself to celebrate—or mourn—one's single status has morphed into something totally new. (Reinforcing the singles theme, it's held on November 11, or 11/11, each year.)

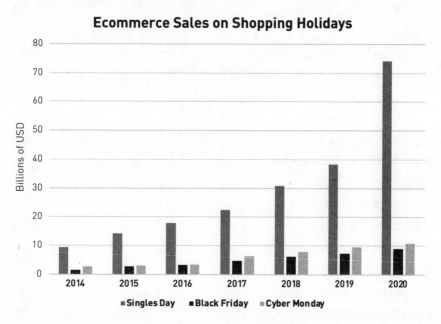

Ecommerce Sales on Shopping Holidays

Sources: Business Insider, Adobe Analytics, Forbes, and KraneShares. Sales figures are approximate and may not reflect all vendors.

According to an article written for *Forbes* in 2019[5] by KraneShares' Brendan Ahern, Alibaba was the first ecommerce platform to monetize Singles' Day starting in 2009. During the final twenty-four hours of 2018's thirty-day 11/11 Global Shopping Festival, Alibaba generated $30.8 billion of gross merchandise volume (GMV). This figure represents nearly five times the reported 2018 online sales for all U.S. retailers on Black Friday. In 2019, Alibaba posted a record-setting $38.4 billion on more than one million purchases, almost all of them made from smartphones.

As Singles' Day has grown into a national celebration over the past decade, the competition has studied Alibaba's playbook, mimicked their formula for success, and in some cases exceeded their capacity to inspire online shopping fervor among citizens of the world's largest internet population.

Evoking Hollywood-grade production quality, the 2018 11/11 Global Shopping Festival culminated around a twenty-four-hour televised and online-streamed gala with celebrity performances and appearances. Original songs (focused on the theme of shopping) were debuted. Alibaba topped all that in 2019 with Taylor Swift.

Swift performed in the televised and livestreamed Countdown Gala in the hours leading up to 11/11. While the 2019 Shopping Festival appeared to follow the same theatrical formula of the 2018 festivities, behind the scenes Alibaba used a new metric for measuring the success of the Global Shopping Festival.

Until 2019, Alibaba used the total value of merchandise sold during its twenty-four-hour flagship event, or GMV, to measure the success of the shopping festival. In 2020, Alibaba decided to focus on customer lifetime value (CLV), which is the net profit a business earns over the duration of a customer relationship.

Alibaba has around a billion customers in China; however, many only transact on one of Alibaba's nine core channels. Using CLV as a success metric, Alibaba aims to increase the number of customers who transact across multiple channels in the Alibaba ecosystem. Customers who transact across more than one channel have a higher retention rate and, more importantly, they provide more value to the company than single-channel customers (users who are both expensive to acquire and have lower retention rates). To achieve this objective, Alibaba focused on growing users in less-developed markets.

Alibaba's new focus on lower-tier markets is a reaction to the Chinese ecommerce upstart Pinduoduo. Pinduoduo's business strategy is aimed at capturing throngs of deal-seeking consumers through "team purchasing." Under this model, users receive discounts by having their friends and family buy the same products as they do. Often located in less-developed markets, Pinduoduo's consumers have a lower average order value with a higher volume of transactions of fast-moving consumer goods such as fresh fruit and toothpaste. We believe the sudden attention Alibaba, and the entire ecommerce industry as a whole, is paying to less-developed markets underscores just how formidable a competitor Pinduoduo has become.

Alibaba's GMV for 2018 was much higher than Pinduoduo's ($853 billion compared to Pinduoduo's $68.6 billion), year-over-year.[6] However, Pinduoduo's GMV grew a staggering 234 percent compared to Alibaba's 19 percent. Marketing tactics include large-scale brand campaigns, targeted advertising, and customized discount coupons aimed at shaping user behavior. Pinduoduo, whose name literally means "together, more and more," got its start by offering discounted produce and other food items through their mobile app. They have since grown their product offering and now represent a formidable force in the ecommerce space.

China consumers tend to mimic the purchases of their friends. For example, women often choose to purchase the same dress as their friends as a sign of status, friendship, and equal footing. The team purchasing approach has also allowed Pinduoduo to penetrate markets that had previously been left out of the broader rise of ecommerce in China. The model means that young people may invite their less tech-savvy friends and even older family members to enter a purchasing group with them, thereby creating new customers from different demographics.

Pinduoduo has surpassed JD.com in terms of market share and is now the second largest ecommerce platform in China behind Alibaba.

To engage less-developed markets for the 11/11 Global Shopping Festival, Alibaba held a concurrent kickoff event in the northeastern city of Harbin. Emulating Pinduoduo's categorical success selling fresh fruit, Alibaba has begun agriculture livestreams showing farmers harvesting produce that users can buy on Alibaba's platform. Turning farm work into an unusual form of entertainment, farmers not only show harvesting to demonstrate freshness, they cut into the fruit to show the ripeness and discuss the taste and smell. In Q2 of 2019, over 70 percent of Alibaba's new annual active consumers came from lower-tier cities. "The success of our focus on less-developed markets in China is reflected in our new customer acquisition growth," said Alibaba Group CMO Chris Tung.

In 2018, JD.com sold $23 billion of goods over an eleven-day Singles' Day campaign. Targeting middle-class customers, JD.com has carved out a niche for itself by selling globally recognized brand names such as Apple, Dell, Dyson, and L'Oréal products. Given that JD.com focuses on higher-end retail, their Singles' Day sales are smaller. However, instead of diluting their core value proposition by selling less expensive merchandise or discounting products beyond profit, they have differentiated their sales strategy by starting an annual anniversary sale shopping event on June 18. Known as the 618 Anniversary Sale. Its success has led Alibaba, Pinduoduo, and other ecommerce platforms to emulate this sale, but instead dubbing it the "618 Mid-Year Shopping Festival."

Success at first was huge—JD.com surpassed Alibaba's Singles' Day GMV during their first event in 2017. However, their first mover advantage was short-lived. Now Pinduoduo and Alibaba both have their own versions of the mid-year shopping festival. Pinduoduo's volume-based strategy garnered 135 million daily active users (DAUs) during last year's 618 Mid-Year Shopping Festival, far exceeding JD.com's 88 million DAUs. Add to that Pinduoduo's lightning-fast 48 percent year-on-year user growth rate, and it is no wonder the whole industry is "Pinduoduofying" their growth strategy.

Alibaba recently reported a 40 percent revenue growth year-over-year. JD.com reported net revenue growth of 42 percent year-over-year. Pinduoduo reported a 169 percent revenue increase year-over-year. With an internet population that has not reached peak adoption and strong competition, we believe ecommerce in China has a strong potential for continued growth.

BAT AND TMD

China's services sector, retail sales, and the expanding universe of publicly traded China internet companies is growing faster than GDP overall (about 8 percent for the technology sector and 6 percent for the economy as a whole in early 2019).[7] This reflects a well-documented phenomenon occurring in China over the past decade that still goes largely unreported. China is shifting from an industrial/export-driven economic model that represented the "old China" economy to a services/domestic consumption-based economic model that characterizes the "new China" economy. In 2013, China's services sector surpassed its industrial sector as the largest contributor to GDP for the first time, and since then, it has continued to steadily outgrow the industrial sector.

CNBC's Jim Cramer coined the term FANG to refer to Facebook, Amazon, Netflix, and Google in 2013. (It's since been amended to FAANG to include Apple.) Since then, acronyms have become a popular tool for defining leaders in the internet sector. In China, the BAT companies (Baidu, Alibaba, and Tencent) have reigned supreme since 2015.

These companies were early entrants to China's internet sector, providing users with search, ecommerce, gaming, and social media. By gaining critical mass relatively early in China's digital evolution, BAT positioned themselves as mainstays of China's digital ecosystem.

Now there is a new acronym representing the "second wave" of China internet giants—born in the era of mobile technology, and all less than ten years old. Toutiao (a unit of ByteDance), Meituan Dianping, and Didi form the new acronym TMD. TMD companies have rapidly grown their valuations to rival those of BAT and offer differentiated services such as personalized information feeds, on-demand delivery, and ride-sharing. The TMD companies have incorporated technology trends such as "super apps," a bundling of functions used by WeChat among others, artificial intelligence (AI) and machine learning algorithms, and have expanded into markets beyond China.

While some see TMD as competition to BAT, in reality, both acronyms reflect the enormous opportunity in China. For over a decade, China has had the largest internet-connected population in the world. However, as a percentage of China's population, this figure is relatively low at only 59.6 percent. This statistic highlights both the size of China's society and the continued potential for growth of its internet population. BAT and TMD are only the first and second of many acronyms to come out of China.

Toutiao

Founded in August 2012, Toutiao had 120 million average daily active users in 2018. By comparison, Twitter, established in 2006, had 100 million average daily active users in 2018. Toutiao, which means "Headlines" in Mandarin, is similar to Twitter in that it provides users with personalized information feeds powered by machine learning algorithms.

While Toutiao is a household name in China, Toutiao's parent company, ByteDance, and social media platform TikTok may be more familiar to Westerners. Specifically launched for markets outside China, TikTok allows users to create and share short lip-sync, comedy, and talent videos. What differentiates TikTok from other Chinese social media apps is that it has penetrated and is thriving in the highly developed U.S. market. TikTok derives 26.5 million of its 500 million monthly active users from the U.S. Within the United States, TikTok's popularity surged after it merged with another ByteDance product, the popular music streaming app musical.ly. In the fourth quarter of 2018, TikTok was the second most downloaded app in the U.S. and was the most downloaded app worldwide for all of 2018.

Given that two-thirds of TikTok users are under thirty, it is likely that if you have kids active on social media, they are already quite familiar with the app. Listed as the most valuable "unicorn" by research firm CB Insights, ByteDance reached a $425 billion valuation in 2021.

Meituan Dianping

Meituan Dianping ("Meituan") is a publicly listed delivery services company obsessed with efficiency. Their primary business objectives are to help people live better through on-demand delivery and help businesses by improving operating efficiency. Initially focused on food delivery, Meituan's super app is a fully integrated app for everything from on-demand delivery to booking flights and transferring money. In the first half of 2018, Meituan facilitated $2.77 billion in food delivery transactions alone for more than 350 million people in 2,800 cities. Using AI-enabled technology, Meituan can determine the optimal delivery route for an order. While this is helpful for the immediate delivery, it also informs and optimizes the routing of future deliveries. On May 20, 2019, Meituan hit a new milestone, surpassing Chinese search engine Baidu in market cap, reaching $45 billion (Baidu's market cap was $41 billion).

As described by Kai-Fu Lee, the former president of Google China, in his book *AI Superpowers* (Houghton Mifflin Harcourt, 2018), the success of Meituan is a prime example of the fierce competition that China's entrepreneurs must go through to succeed.

Back in 2011, Groupon entered the China market through a partnership with Tencent and saw its valuation skyrocket to over $1 billion in just sixteen months. The concept of a group buying company seemed tailor-made for China, and while Groupon was the front-runner, many Chinese startups subsequently started popping up.

By the time Groupon went public, China was home to more than five thousand different group buying companies, one of which was Meituan. Its founder, Wang Xing, had built two companies in the past and sharpened his skills beyond computer engineering to serial entrepreneurship.

Meituan pioneered an automated payment mechanism that got money into the hands of businesses quicker. The stability of Meituan's payment platform inspired loyalty among its customers, and Wang leveraged it to build out larger networks of exclusive partnerships.

By 2013, Groupon shut down its China business and virtually all the other startups collapsed, leaving just three companies in the space—Meituan, Dianping, and Nuomi. In sharp contrast to Groupon, Wang expanded Meituan's lines of business and reshaped its core products. As the new consumer wave began to take hold, Wang pivoted his company to participate in the fast-growing online-to-offline (O2O) business trend. Meituan merged with Dianping in 2015 to form an O2O behemoth, and Nuomi quickly changed business strategies, eventually being bought by iQiyi in May 2018.

Didi Chuxing

Most people are familiar with or have used a ride-sharing service like Uber or Lyft. However, as mentioned earlier, Didi Chuxing, or "Didi," is unlike American ride-sharing services. While Uber and Lyft compete for market dominance in the U.S., Didi dominates the China market, controlling 91 percent of the ride-sharing market in addition to having a significant presence outside China. Didi is a trailblazer in their pursuit to become "a global leader in the transportation automotive technology revolution."

Didi has already fundamentally changed driver and consumer behavior in China. Today, it is virtually impossible to hail a cab on the street without using a ride-share app. Didi is also expanding globally through acquisition and market entry. Didi has set up operations in Taiwan, Japan, Australia, Brazil, and Mexico. Didi has expanded its mandate beyond ride-sharing to include car insurance, auto finance and financial services, enterprise technology services, and investing in the research and development of autonomous vehicles. Didi was listed as the second-largest unicorn startup on CB Insights' unicorn list, reaching a nearly $60 billion valuation since the company was founded in June 2012. It raised $4.4 billion in a closely watched IPO on Wall Street in June 2021.

iQiyi

Outside the TMD acronym but knocking on the door is iQiyi, one of China's top video streaming companies, often referred to as the "Netflix of China."

iQiyi has risen to the top by innovating the Chinese online video space. In 2015, there were not many quality films being made for online distribution, and those that were had minimal resources and low budgets. But there was a surge in quality online movie production in 2016, when 2,500 online movies were produced, up from 689 titles the year before. Suddenly online video became one of the fastest growing verticals in the China internet space and now accounts for 25 percent of total time spent online.

iQiyi saw this opportunity in 2015 and led China's charge in hosting original content online. What separated iQiyi from its competitors was its unique business model with regard to hosting content. The company offered a 50-50 revenue split to titles that met certain quality standards. iQiyi's focus shifted to quality over quantity, and its revenue and subscriptions similarly increased. In May 2015, iQiyi had only 5 million paying subscribers, but by June 2018, that number had risen by more than ten times to 66.2 million. By the end of 2017, iQiyi ranked first among Chinese video platforms with 463 million monthly active users, versus Tencent Video's 458 million and Alibaba-backed Youku's 374 million.

iQiyi also utilizes Baidu's world-class artificial intelligence (AI) research to improve the efficiency of its operations. CEO Tim Gong Yu in December 2017 described the benefits of Baidu's AI, saying, "We're able to predict the box-office potential of a theatrical film release with a pretty high degree of accuracy, which helps us determine how much to spend on licensing before the film has come out . . . But this is just the beginning: AI will dramatically change the media and entertainment industry over the next 5 to 10 years."[8] iQiyi's access to cutting-edge AI research and technology will likely give it an edge and allow for it to optimize its business operations better than its competitors.

BRANDS TO WATCH

With continuing innovation in robotics, AI, facial recognition, and much more, other budding companies will emerge to serve Chinese consumers, especially city dwellers. It's all in the plan.

Many companies in this sector are making great strides, and the following list is ever-changing. Here are just a few to watch.

Trip.com provides search and full booking services for flights, hotels, trains, car rentals, tours, and more to China's travelers. The company provides booking services abroad as well as within China. The firm has big ambitions outside the China market.

Tencent Music operates a music streaming platform. TM's platform offers livestreaming, uploading, and socializing services around the music industry. The platform offers media coming out of China and abroad. The music streaming service is comparable to Spotify or Apple Music in the United States. TME has begun to invest in original content as well.

The company 58.com operates a multisite platform that offers job-search, business-directory, real estate marketplace, and peer-to-peer marketing services. The company offers a diverse array of products in its peer-to-peer marketplace, from real estate to general consumer products. The company has also launched new business initiatives including Zhuan, which is a marketplace for secondhand goods, and 58 Town, which has the ability to cater to small-town needs. Users can post information relevant only to a certain small geographic area. This service is poised to speed 58.com's entry into growth markets in lower-tier cities and rural areas, similar to what Nextdoor is doing in the U.S.

We will next look at China's environment and how technology is working to make it better.

CHAPTER ELEVEN
A Green China

TURNING GRAY TO GREEN

"Heaven does not speak, and it alternates the four seasons; Earth does not speak, and it nurtures all things." China's President Xi Jinping shared a Chinese poem, often attributed to Confucius, espousing the virtues of protecting the natural environment during the UN's Climate Ambition Summit on Saturday, December 13, 2020. President Xi went on to say that "Earth is our only shared home" as he renewed China's commitment to the principles of the Paris Agreement on climate change and announced new environmental goals for China by 2030 focused on the renewable energy industry, especially solar and wind.[1]

One keen listener was Xiabing Su, who we met earlier. She works for KraneShares as a cultural analyst, now based in Shanghai after schooling in New York and producing articles and videos on the significant changes happening in China. She is one of my key employees, helping me understand not only the China Dream, but also the bridges between the U.S. and China. Her personal recollections of her childhood in Lanzhou, a city in the northwest part of China, and adult life in New York vividly paint a picture of China's environmental problems and its progress.

"I was born in Lanzhou, a city in the northwest part of China. One of the memories from my childhood was the dust flying in winter. Sometimes, the air was full of the smell of the dirt and I couldn't help but to cough. Masks were not only used in the hospitals or for those who were sick. In the winter, you could see lots of people cover their mouths and noses with masks and big scarfs, walking on the street hurriedly.

"I remember once a sandstorm with strong wind. It happened while I was having classes in my middle school. When the dust came, I felt like the world suddenly changed its face. The sky turned from gray to yellow and the wind was howling. The half of the playground outside the window disappeared into a yellow mist.

"The scene was similar to some cyberpunk movies I watched after I grew up. Ryan Gosling looks pretty cool when he is walking in the sandstorm to trace his origins in the film *Blade Runner 2049*, but trust me, sandstorms in real life are just terrifying. My teacher told us sandstorms often occurred in places with an arid climate and lack of vegetation, and that's the main geographical feature of northwestern China. However, some human activities, like man-made overgrazing and deforestation, worsen the situation. The gas from cars and factory pollution made the air even more unbearable.

"I realized my mood was very easily affected by the weather and air. I wanted to leave the city and find a blue skyline. I wanted to be calmed by the embrace of trees. I did leave, by choosing a college closer to the sea, and decided to pursue my master's degree in the U.S. and stayed in New York for a while.

"The place I loved most in New York was Central Park. I was amazed that in one of the world's busiest cities there could be a peaceful habitat right in the center. With the nourishment of the natural habitat, people can unload their worries and enjoy the presence by just walking along the lakeside, reading under trees, or having a picnic on the large lawn. This was my ideal—a perfect balance between human and nature. A connection with nature can help me refresh and become more creative. When I saw people's smiling faces while their babies were crawling on the grass, no matter what their ethnicities, I believe this is not only my dream, but a common dream that we all share: a desire for harmony and happiness.

"I left the U.S. and went back to my hometown in the second half of 2020. Just spending another winter in Lanzhou after seven years away, I realized many tremendous changes have happened, and the environmental improvements are too significant to ignore. The horrible sandstorms had become history, and the sky turned blue even in the winter. We are still wearing masks—not because of the dust but only due to COVID-19.

"I'm so glad that we are finding solutions for a better balance between development and environment. For many years, China has been implementing desertification prevention and control and returning farmland to forest projects in the western and northern regions. I saw the results. Even more, my dad told me many industrial factories that had been polluting the air and water have been remediated by local government. Power stations have gone through the process of ultralow emission retrofits. People are encouraged to use green energy cars since a green car license is not as restricted as those for gasoline-powered cars.

"I guess knowing what we could do, as well as our limitations, is rational. I will never expect Lanzhou to be turned into a city like those in the wet areas of China. The winter will still be cold, dry, and bold, but after what I witnessed, I'm confident that the future will be even better. President Xi said China will reduce carbon emissions to zero by 2060, and China's forest coverage rate will reach and stabilize above 26 percent.

"I'm excited to witness this transformation. I do hope my country can take more responsibility in global issues like environmental change due to its large size. I'm also excited to witness our planet becoming cleaner and healthier. I only want to see *Blade Runner* in the cinema, not in reality."

I am both touched and impressed by Su's story. I'm a huge fan of anything that improves our environment, from cleaner water to cleaner air. I'm also a big fan of quieter, less-polluting cars, and think the worldwide movement to electric vehicles is very positive.

China's economic growth has come with a corresponding increase in automobile ownership, construction projects, and energy consumption, particularly coal consumption.

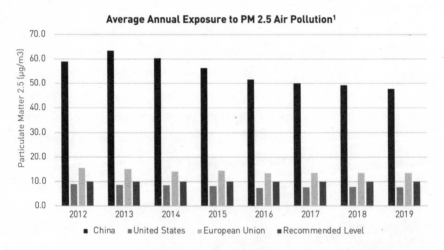

Average Annual Exposure to PM 2.5 Air Pollution[1]

Data from China Water Risk State of Ecology & Environment Report Review 2020 as of 6/18/2021.

As China's economy has shifted away from its dependency on manufacturing, it is now better equipped to deal with environmental concerns. China's economy has become more balanced in recent years as services surpassed industrials as the largest contributor to GDP. The U.S. underwent a similar shift from the 1950s to the 1970s, and today the percentage of U.S. GDP generated from services far exceeds that of industry.

China's focus on environmental protection has strengthened following the formation of the Ministry of Environmental Protection in July 2008, superseded by the Ministry of Ecology and Environment. The goal of the government is to achieve 50 percent commercial green building certification by 2022. If met, China will represent half of the world's green-building floor space.

While China is the world leader in total renewable energy, at 31 percent of global capacity, there is still significant room for growth. In terms of per capita renewable power output, China produces less than half the capacity of the United States and one-third the capacity of the European Union. China has proven highly capable of achieving its ambitious targets for increasing renewable energy capacity. By the end of 2015, China exceeded the goal it set for total renewable energy capacity in the twelfth Five-Year Plan by 11.8 percent. Total renewable energy capacity increased 12.2 percent year-over-year from 2017 to 2018.

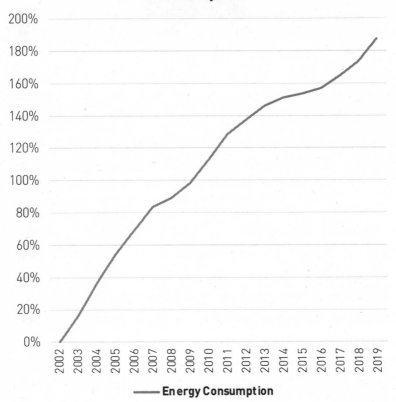

Annual Increase in Energy Consumption

Energy Consumption

Data from China's National Bureau of Statistics 2020,
Total Consumption of Energy and Its Composition.

The year 2020 was a good one for China's cleantech companies with electric vehicles and solar and wind companies leading the way. Investors were continuously pricing in higher demand targets driven by stronger than expected adoption and favorable government regulations. Furthermore, Tesla announced in September 2020 that it expects to cut its battery cost by almost 56 percent, another step toward achieving grid-parity with internal combustion engine (ICE) automobiles.

China's government is spending billions of dollars in subsidizing electric car manufacturers to stimulate growth and ensure that electric cars are affordable to average Chinese citizens.

Every time I stroll along the sidewalks on any busy Beijing street, what strikes me first is something that mainly isn't there: noise.

There are dozens of small vans and rickshaw-like vehicles jostling each other for position among the steady stream of cars, but almost all of them are silent, battery-driven vehicles. Long gone are the polluting putt-putts that used to rule Beijing traffic. It's quiet but welcome.

China's most important auto company is FAW Group. This China state-owned automotive manufacturing company is headquartered in Changchun, China, which is the capital of Jilin province. FAW, meaning "First Automobile Works," became China's first automobile manufacturer in 1958, when it unveiled the nation's first domestically produced passenger car, the Hongqi. Chairman Mao founded FAW, and the Hongqi brand has since been a symbol of national pride throughout China. In 1965, Hongqi was declared the official government car for senior government officials and foreign guests. President Xi currently drives in a Hongqi.

Today, FAW is a Global Fortune 100 Company with a strong focus on electric vehicles for the consumer market in China. As provinces in China become 100 percent EV through government policy, Hongqi will be well-positioned.

Industry projections say electric vehicles (EVs) will reach parity with internal combustion engine cars in most countries soon.[2] China is aiming for 40 percent of all vehicles sold in the country to be electric by 2030. Less than 3 percent of the fourteen million cars sold in the United States were electric in 2020. There is a lot of potential for change before we reach peak adoption of electric and future vehicles. It's becoming clear that China will ultimately dominate the EV revolution.

Automakers are globalized companies, and many are looking to expand into other important markets, especially China. China is already the largest electric vehicle market in the world, accounting for 40 percent of global EV sales. Tesla is already making cars in mainland China. It is joined by other companies that are partnering with electric vehicle manufacturers, including Daimler with Build Your Dreams (BYD), and BMW with Great Wall Motors.

China auto production is closely tied to environmental concerns. China produces about twenty-five million cars a year, the most in the world, and by 2035, 60 percent, or fifteen million, will be electric. In addition, advancements in power storage technology and production methods have made electric vehicles increasingly more cost-competitive with traditional automobiles.

Tesla's entrance into the S&P 500 Index in December 2020 signaled the arrival of the EV ecosystem as a bona fide sector that investors can no longer ignore. Cost reduction, stricter emissions regulations, government incentives, and the rollout of new and affordable models are bringing EVs within reach of the mass consumer. In 2021, EVs finally appear poised to move out of the realm of the future and onto the driveways of the masses. It's a key part of the China Dream.

EVs are exhibiting "hockey stick growth" in terms of both sales and stock prices. A dramatic, COVID-infected 2020 began with a drop in EV sales but ended with a sales boom. We believe the upward trend will continue.

Despite the pandemic and a slumping global automotive industry, EV sales achieved 43 percent growth from 2019 to 2020, mostly due to strong adoption in Europe and China.[3]

In China, EV sales recovered during the fourth quarter, registering positive year-on-year growth with sales totaling 1.36 million units for 2020.

EV Unit Sales and Growth

	China	EU	US
2019	1,189,290	562,000	325,710
2020	1,366,000	1,367,000	329,000
2021 E	1,800,000	1,900,000	576,000
2021 E Growth	31.77%	38.99%	75.08%

Source: CLSA and Macquarie as of 12/31/2020.

China's government quickly reinstated EV subsidies in 2020 and continues to encourage local governments to relax car permit quotas for EVs.[4] In many of the largest metropolitan areas in China there are strict limits imposed by local governments on the number of license plates that can be issued in order to reduce congestion. But China now mandates that such limits will not apply to the issuance of "green license plates," which are issued for electric vehicles, driving sales.

Approximately 75 million internal combustion engine (ICE) vehicles were sold worldwide in 2019 compared to 3.26 million EVs in 2020, the best year yet for EV sales. EV sales are far from catching up with ICE vehicle sales, but technological improvements make EVs more economical and thereby more palatable to the mass market.

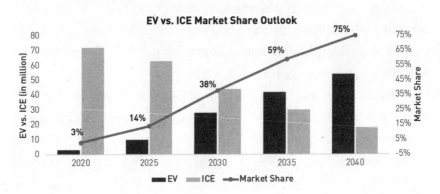

Source: Macquarie. Data as of December 2020.

In an April 2021 report[5] McKinsey highlighted "the irresistible momentum behind clean, electric, connected mobility." An earlier McKinsey study found 37 percent of respondents said they would consider switching car brands for better connectivity. In China, the percentage was even higher at 57 percent. The automobile looks increasingly like a smartphone.

The quest for autonomous vehicles is being pursued in China by companies from various sectors. Tech giants like Baidu are leveraging their experience with data processing, artificial intelligence, and mapping to produce and improve self-driving car technology. Baidu is planning on leveraging the information gathered from its Apollo program, the first open-source simulator for autonomous vehicle developers, sharing information in order to mass-produce self-driving vehicles as soon as 2022.

Driverless vehicles are essentially mobile supercomputers. They require sensors, radars, and incredibly powerful processing chips that run complex AI technology in order to operate.

Especially in China, the advent of future mobility technology is blurring the lines between traditional auto manufacturers and technology companies while creating new markets for producers of processing chips, batteries, and their raw material inputs.

Baidu's Panda Auto has the world's first fully electric fleet of shared mobility vehicles. The company has over 15,000 electric cars and over 2.1 million registered users as of November 2017.

Chinese automaker BYD (Build Your Dreams) is one of the world's largest electric vehicle manufacturers and has sold vehicles for use as public buses to the cities of London and Long Beach, CA. Warren Buffett invested $230 million into BYD in 2008.

It's always good to follow Warren's advice. His investment is an endorsement of the fact that China is doing groundbreaking research in this field, as in many others.

One of the commitments announced during the UN's Climate Ambition Summit was to bring total solar and wind capacity to 1,200 gigawatts by 2030 from the current approximate level of 455GW capacity (227GW wind and 228GW solar). To meet these goals, China will have to initiate an average of 70–80GW of new solar and wind installations per year over the next nine years.

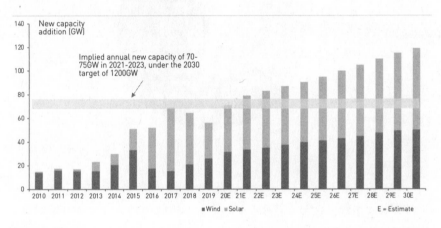

Source: CLSA. Data of December 2020.

Analysts believe these targets will be overachieved. Although China is now the world's largest producer of renewable energy, solar and wind remain only a tiny portion of China's energy generation mix (3 percent of energy is generated by solar versus 6 percent by wind). They are expected to take a more prominent role in the next ten years. Sixty-two percent of China's electricity generation is from coal-fired plants, 18 percent from hydro, and 5 percent from nuclear. Globally, only 1.1 percent of energy is produced by solar and 2.2 percent by wind compared to roughly 85 percent by fossil fuels (oil, coal, and gas).

Energy Mix in 2019

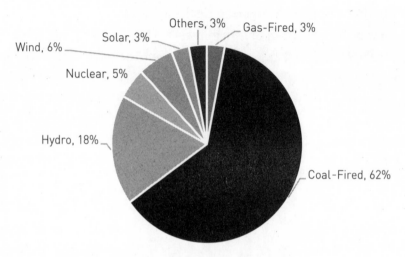

Data from China National Energy Administration (NEA).

Solar and wind are the favorites in the race of renewables. The price of producing energy using solar is now equal to or below the current price per unit of energy without government subsidies in many regions.

According to Bloomberg, the global average cost of solar energy has declined by more than 80 percent since 2010, and we could see another 25 percent drop by 2025.[6] The cost reduction has been due to two factors: First is the continuous drop in the price of all solar upstream materials such as silicon, wafer, and glass. The other reason for the price reduction is innovation across the solar photovoltaic (PV) product supply chain. These innovations include higher quality silicon, bigger solar wafers, more efficient solar cells, and bifacial modules that can gather light on both sides. According to China's Photovoltaic Industry Association (CPIA), solar cell efficiency could increase by another 1 to 2 percent by

2025, a significant gain.[7] China has been leading the way in solar power innovation with companies held within our KGRN ETF directing the charge, such as GCL-Poly Energy, LONGI, JinkoSolar, and Xinyi Solar.

There has been great excitement for renewable energy over the past few years as many countries have renewed their commitment to a greener planet. However, economic and social barriers remain significant as countries try to perform a balancing act between moving to renewables and supporting those employed by the fossil fuel industry. As the cost of renewable energy falls and governments increase their support for the sector, innovative companies in the space are poised to benefit. China currently leads the world in cost reduction, public support, and implementation, providing a long-term catalyst for the country's clean energy firms.

We at KraneShares were proud to introduce a fund investing in China's climate change initiatives at the NYSE on July 30, 2020, and hosted the Biden administration's now Climate Head, John Kerry, at the bell ringing ceremony.

We were pleased that Secretary Kerry endorsed our KraneShares Global Carbon (KRBN) ETF, an exchange-traded fund tracking the three most robust markets for carbon credits.

The fund lets everybody invest in the carbon credit market, one of the chief mechanisms for limiting greenhouse gas emissions under the Paris Climate Accord Kerry helped negotiate in 2015. The ETF may help set a single worldwide price for carbon—a crucial step to build on the Paris Agreement.

Before becoming the Biden administration's chief climate advisor in 2021, Kerry was an advisor to Climate Finance Partners, cofounded by Eron Bloomgarden and Richmond Mayo-Smith. New York–based Krane Funds Advisors runs the ETF with Climate Finance Partners as a subadvisor, and we regard it as one of the most important things we do.

At the NYSE meeting, I said that the best way to curb pollution and save the planet is to put a price on carbon emissions. China is starting an emissions trading system this year that will probably be added to the index. A lot of countries are launching carbon credit markets. As those exchanges become more liquid, they will be good candidates to add into our carbon fund.

Progress toward a cleaner environment goes hand in hand with the health of China's population. We'll look at the big changes in health care, often driven by technology, in the next chapter.

CHAPTER TWELVE
A Healthy China

GETTING HEALTHY IN A HURRY

As the COVID-19 pandemic illustrated, health challenges can be daunting and arise quickly. The China Dream will depend on vastly expanding quality health care to everyone. And as we've seen throughout this book, advances in health care are being made using the latest technology, mostly China-made. Dozens of new and some old companies are dominating the field. We'll look at a few of them later in this chapter.

The demand for quality health care is rising rapidly. Like most of the challenges China faces, the country has decided to tackle this with technology and innovation.

Rising demand from wealthier Chinese people seeking quality care and diverse services has led to increased privatization of hospitals to match demand. In 2015, China's 15,570 private hospitals outnumbered its 12,871 public hospitals for the first time.

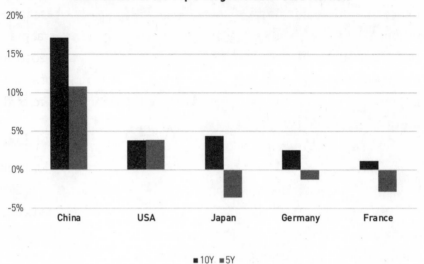

Growth Rate of the Top 5 Largest Health Care Markets

■ 10Y ■ 5Y

Source: World Health Organization.

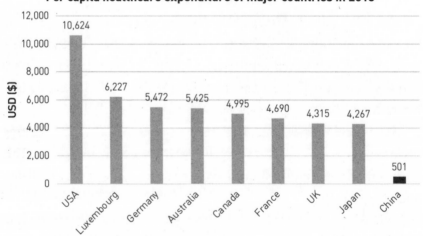

Per capita healthcare expenditure of major countries in 2018

Source: World Health Organization.

The "Healthy China 2030" policy outlines the government's plans to upgrade the standards and quality of service in primary care institutions. The government set a goal to have five qualified general practitioners available for every ten thousand residents in China by 2030, in an effort to control high medical expenditures. Establishment of a medical network and referral system is geared toward reducing overcrowding in China's largest hospitals.

First a quick word about traditional Chinese medicine. As with much innovation here, the health care sector has been careful to tailor itself to Chinese tradition and needs. Traditional Chinese medicine (TCM) has a rich two-thousand-year history encompassing herbal medicine, acupuncture, massage, and dietetics. In recent years, TCM has enjoyed a modern resurgence championed by President Xi Jinping. In December 2016, China's State Council issued the "Strategic Plan on the Development of Traditional Chinese Medicine," making the development of TCM a national strategy. The policy emphasizes promoting a balance between Western medicine and TCM practices.

The TCM industry grew by 20 percent in 2017, earning a total of $130 billion, or one-third of total medical industry output. Currently, there are about 482,000 TCM practitioners in China. By 2020, the government had also sought to register one hundred TCM products and set up fifty international TCM cooperation model centers.

TCM practitioners emphasize preventative medicine and treating diseases before they occur through healthy living and proper diets. This is especially important in China, which has increasing obesity, diabetes, and smoking rates.

One of China's oldest pharmaceutical companies focused on Chinese traditional medicine is Yunnan Baiyao, which means "Yunnan's white drug," a reference to the company's main product, Baiyao, which is a white powder made primarily of ginseng and used to stop bleeding. The company has since expanded to a broad range of pharmaceutical products, including pills, toothpaste, and shampoo.

Obviously the COVID-19 pandemic was and is a major challenge for China, as well as the world. While China emerged from the pandemic in late 2020, it caused some profound and lasting changes, which we detailed in a report during the course of 2020.[1] Again, there is a lot of information here, with details of many companies. Consider it a collection of potential investment ideas.

"China's population quickly took to a new stay-at-home lifestyle. Employees started relying more heavily on office collaboration platforms to work remotely from home, and students turned to China's vast selection of online education courses to continue with their studies. To put this in perspective, daily active users of Tencent's Enterprise WeChat office application have increased tenfold since February 10th [2020]; and Alibaba's communication platform, Ding Talk, has reached its highest levels in five years, with 200 million daily active users.

"During the height of the virus and particularly in more affected areas, locals adopted innovative ways of dealing with their new normal. Public buses were converted into mobile food markets, everyday items were creatively transformed into makeshift masks, and some companies like JD.com began using drones to drop off items direct to residents' doorsteps. One woman captured her inventive at-home delivery technique on video: She remotely drives a toy car, installed with cameras and a loudspeaker, to pick up steamed buns at a nearby shop.

"Even though the virus has had a significant impact on the Chinese population and their day-to-day lives, we believe that videos such as these reflect the strength and resiliency of China's people and businesses.

"China has historically underinvested in health care, but it is reasonable to expect an upgrade to its health care spending plans following this public health crisis. In recent years, there has been an increased focus on expanding the number of China's drug development facilities, an effort that has established China as one of the world's top outsourcing destinations for biomanufacturing second only to the U.S. We expect further growth as companies within China's pharmaceutical sector continue to broaden their biomanufacturing footprint and accelerate their own drug development capabilities.

"This outbreak may be a strong catalyst for growth, particularly for companies involved in health care IT, pharmaceuticals, and traditional Chinese medicine, which have had an outsized role in combating the virus.

"To ease the burden of already overcrowded hospitals, leading online health care providers Alibaba Health and Ping An 'Good Doctor' began offering their telemedicine services free of charge to encourage anyone with minor, non-coronavirus illnesses to seek treatment through their online doctor portals. These health care IT platforms, which allow patients to connect with doctors via app, have vastly expanded the reach and capabilities of China's health care system. Recently, leading online health care providers have seen a drastic growth in users. Alibaba Health had more than four hundred thousand visitors from Hubei province alone just two days after offering its no-fee service, and Ping An 'Good Doctor' has seen ten times the number of newly registered users since the onset of the outbreak.

"Even China's top search engine, Baidu, entered the health care space, providing a service where users could monitor whether people on the same flight or train have tested positive for the virus. Many companies have experimented with ways to diagnose the coronavirus more accurately, but Baidu made great headway by creating an AI analysis system that reduced the detection time of the virus from nearly an hour to less than half a minute.

"With supplies of protective gear selling out in cities throughout China, it became especially critical that companies found solutions to supply-chain roadblocks. The Chinese conglomerate Shanghai Fosun International was quick to execute a global emergency contingency plan to expedite medical supplies from its branches in Germany, Portugal, and Japan, becoming among the first to import hundreds of thousands of face masks and hazmat suits to the most affected regions within China.

"People have become reliant on existing drugs to not only treat symptoms of the coronavirus but also for stockpiling supplies at home. Many of China's pharma companies have been integral to aiding this current crisis through both drug research and provisions. Jiangsu Hengrui Medicine, China's largest pharma company, sent $400,000 worth of its pegfilgrastim drug, which targets regrowth of white blood cells, directly to Wuhan in its first round of donations. At the same time, Jiangsu Hengrui's stock rose 35 percent over a one-year period.

"In addition to pharmaceuticals, traditional Chinese medicine (TCM) is being used both at home and in hospitals to alleviate symptoms. Many have stocked up on over-the-counter Chinese cold medicine, like China Resources' '999 Cold Remedy' and Beijing TongRenTang's liquid herbal formulas. At hospitals, of the eighty clinical trials on potential treatments for the coronavirus, approximately fifteen incorporate TCM practices. With people turning to more holistic remedies both for preventive care as well as to supplement their treatments, TCM may also see revenues increase.

"We believe that there is a positive growth trend developing for China health care in the wake of the coronavirus. Health care in China has room for growth as it continues to develop. We believe that this public health crisis will prompt an upgrading to its health care spending plans. Moreover, China is already leading in the adoption of digital health care technology. Health care IT platforms have gained a considerable number of new users recently as people delayed hospital visits to avoid coronavirus exposure. We believe the current outbreak could serve as a catalyst for advancing research and technology across various China health care subsectors and may offer long-term growth potential for China health care as a whole."[2]

Through reforms, the Chinese government has been successful in improving quality, affordability, and accessibility to care for its citizens, and it is entirely determined to build a robust and competitive domestic health care industry. We believe China's health care sector today is akin to its technology and fintech sectors in 2013. Since then, these sectors have made great leaps and beaten expectations.

For health care IT, we believe the pandemic will prove to be an inflection point for the industry, resulting in accelerated user adoption and favorable policy. Online health care is an exciting growth theme that combines health care with technology. In August 2019, China's National Healthcare Security Administration (NHSA) issued a new guidance to include internet diagnosis and treatment into the social insurance, and officially removed the ban on online prescription drug sales.

The guidance was aimed to provide Chinese citizens in rural areas with easy access to quality health care without having to travel for hours. Following the COVID-19 outbreak, the NHSA further stressed the importance of telemedicine in two separate documents, suggesting favorable policy for online health care is being expedited. Several cities and local governments jumped on the bandwagon and took the major step of adding the services to the social insurance reimbursement list.

Ping An Good Doctor and Alibaba Health both saw user registration jump more than tenfold in the days following the COVID-19 outbreak. Ping An Good Doctor currently has over 369 million registered users and over 67 million monthly active users. Online consultations are expected to grow from 3 percent to 20 percent in 2026. Telemedicine shortens wait times from hours to minutes, lowers medical costs, and expands access to twenty-four hours a day, seven days a week.

Alibaba Health is the largest online health care ecommerce platform. It is the health care flagship company of Alibaba. Market size of retail pharmacy is expected to grow by 15 percent per year between now and 2023. Also, Alibaba Health's delivery track record during the pandemic has been impeccable.

Other beneficiaries from the pandemic were medical device companies as demand for ventilators and vital equipment surged. Mindray was one of the main suppliers for the two emergency specialty hospitals constructed in ten days in Wuhan: the Huoshenshan Hospital (1,000 beds) and Leishenshan Hospital (1,600 beds).

In addition, there was more ICU equipment demand for middle-tier public hospitals which were already underinvested. ICU beds in China constitute 5 percent of total beds compared to 15 percent in developed countries. We expect the government to impose higher standards for hospitals as a result of the pandemic, driving further demand for medical devices. Furthermore, Mindray and Jiangsu Yuyue Medical benefited substantially as overseas demand for ventilators reached ten times its normal level. The two companies received FDA approvals in March and early April 2020 to sell ventilators in the U.S. China's health care sector may have an opportunity to significantly ramp up its global business because of the outbreak. Mindray is one of the largest medical device manufacturers in China. The company's products include patient monitoring & life support (PMLS) including ventilators (38 percent of total sales); in vitro diagnostic, or IVD (35 percent of total sales); and medical imaging (24 percent of total sales).

China's health care sector can be complex and difficult to understand. It is much different from the system in the U.S., which is driven by the next big milestone or blockbuster drug and high pricing. In China, health care is a long-term growth theme driven by high volume and the growing unmet needs of an aging population and a rising middle class, who are demanding and are willing to pay for better treatments and care.

The health care sector consists of three main industries: the upstream, middlestream, and downstream industries. The upstream industry includes pharma manufacturers and contract organizations who assist pharmaceuticals with discovery, research, development, manufacturing, and marketing.

China has the second largest Rx industry in the world with RMB 1.3 trillion in sales and is expected to grow to RMB 3.5 trillion by 2030. The industry is currently in transition from generic-focused to innovative in the form of biologic drugs and targeted therapies for autoimmune, oncology, and cardiovascular diseases. Currently, biological drugs have 17 percent market share compared to 51.4 percent for chemical drugs and 31.5 percent for traditional Chinese medicine.

The transition has been supported by the government through reforms, a shortened drug approval process, and improved patient access to novel drugs. While the biotech market in China is still at an early stage, it is expected to drive sector growth for years. The largest pharma companies include Jiangsu Hengrui Med, CSPC Pharmaceuticals Group, and Sino Biopharmaceutical. While Hengrui is ahead in the transition to innovative drugs with multiple oncology drugs launched and a deep pipeline of oncology, autoimmune, and diabetes drugs currently in phase III trials, Sino Bio and CSPC Pharma are not too far behind; however, their reliance on generic drugs remains substantial. Over the past five years, pharmaceuticals and distributors have lost sector share in favor of biotechnology, life science, services, and medical equipment industries.

Given the high demand for new drugs, contract organizations are also prospering and we believe that these companies currently have the best growth prospects. Pharmaceuticals are shifting much of the research and development to contract research organizations (CROs), contract manufacturing organizations (CMOs), and contract development manufacturing organizations (CDMOs). Contract organizations include WuXi Biologics and WuXi AppTech.

These companies allow pharma to save substantial amounts of money that they would otherwise spend on building labs and manufacturing facilities for unproven drugs. Pharma companies continue to increase their yearly R&D budget, which bodes very well for contract organizations.

The middlestream industry is responsible for distributing the drugs. This includes companies such as Shanghai Pharma, Sinopharm, and China Resource Pharma (the Big Three). They have nationwide warehouses and networks that cover hospitals at all levels in addition to deep pockets to withstand large accounts receivable and long recovery cycles.

The downstream industry provides services and includes hospitals, community health clinics, and pharmacies. Unlike in the U.S., most people in China go to hospitals to see doctors and most of the drugs are dispensed through hospitals. Public hospitals tend to attract the best doctors in the country, lured by academic resources and connections. A new pocket of growth in China's health care sector is private hospitals such as AIER Hospitals, which tend to have higher quality care, especially for complex medical needs.

Tying it all together at the bottom are the payers, and that is the Chinese government for the most part. There are three major public insurance companies that cover more than 98 percent of people in China.

Through these insurance companies, the government can dictate which drug makes it on the reimbursement list and at what price through multiple transparent mechanisms. Public insurance covers basic needs, and patients face significant wait time. Private insurance is an emerging industry for those who are willing to pay more. It covers more complex care needs and can provide patients with better arrangements.

Hengrui, a leading pharma company, focuses on developing, manufacturing, and marketing pharmaceutical products mainly in the fields of oncology, surgical drugs, and contrasting agents, among others. Over the past decade, Hengrui has been able to generate strong and stable growth as they successfully continue to transition from generic-focused to innovative drugs.

Hengrui finished 2019 strong with good progress in its pipeline. Hengrui has been executing on the vision of innovation and globalization to diversify and mitigate the pricing risk from its generic drug business due to China's national rollout of centralized procurement. COVID-19's impact is manageable but may cause a two to three months' delay in patient enrollment in certain clinical trials.

The top contract discovery research marketing organization (CDRMO) in China and fourth largest globally is WuXi. WuXi helps pharmaceutical companies cut costs by offering outsourcing services in the fields of discovery, research, development, and marketing of drugs. It is a one-stop service provider offering end-to-end solutions in biologics discovery. They have one of the largest teams of scientists, in addition to a presence in Europe and the U.S. We believe the company is well positioned to reap the benefits of increasing demand for biological drugs in China.

WuXi Biologic's WuXi AppTec is a global tech platform that offers a portfolio of medical R&D resources to shorten the lag time in biomedical discovery and innovative development.

A comprehensive end-to-end innovative drug R&D services provider to biotechnology and pharmaceutical companies globally, WuXi AppTec assists global drug companies with discovery, research, development, and marketing. The company has operations in China, the U.S., and Germany.

WuXi had a strong 2019. The company has been growing at 27 percent CAGR over the past five years and management is confident they can maintain similar growth for the next few years. The company saw a limited impact from COVID-19, as most of its business in China resumed operations on February 11, 2020. Only its Wuhan operations remained closed until March 11 of that year.

CSPC has three major business segments, including innovative drugs, common generic drugs, and bulk drugs. CSPC focuses on the developing, manufacturing, and marketing of medicines and pharmaceutical-related products. CSPC Pharma has a robust generic drug lineup and a strong pipeline of innovative drugs. CSPC is in the process of transitioning to innovative drugs.

CSPC had another 25 percent top line growth year in 2019, driven by strong sales of its key products of generic and innovative drugs. In 2019, ten products were granted drug registration approval in China, sixteen products granted clinical trial approval, and seventeen products passed the consistency evaluation of generic drugs. CSPC is expected to maintain 20–25 percent growth for the next couple of years. However, to unleash the next phase of growth, CSPC must make progress in its innovative drugs pipeline.

China's third largest pharma company and industry leader for liver disease drugs, Sino Bio, researches, develops, produces, and sells biopharmaceutical products in therapeutic categories with promising potential across a variety of biopharmaceutical and chemical medicines.

The firm's newly launched innovative drugs, especially in oncology, are promising and expected to drive future growth.

The company continues to transition to innovation-driven drugs with expected label expansions for newly launched oncology drugs and new launches in 2021.

Innovent Biologics is a leading integrated biotechnology company in China. The company is a fully integrated platform with the ability to be self-reliant in research, development, manufacturing, and commercialization of innovative drugs. The company has strategic partnerships with global companies such as Eli Lilly and Incyte. Innovent recently launched its first oncology drug in China in collaboration with Eli Lilly.

China is one of the fastest growing major health care markets in the world with a five-year compound annual growth rate of 11 percent, compared to just 4 percent in the United States, and negative 4 percent in Japan.[3] China is the second largest health care market globally with total health care expenditures of about $930 billion in 2020.[4] In 2011, China adopted universal health care with 95 percent of China's population gaining access to health care services.

The huge market has attracted global pharmaceutical giants such as Pfizer and Astra-Zeneca. Several market-friendly policies have been introduced encouraging joint ventures between multinational companies and domestic companies. In 2015, the China Food and Drug Administration (CFDA) issued "Opinions on Reforming the Review and Approval System for Drugs and Medical Devices," which set policies aimed toward increasing efficiency and transparency of drug review and approval processes, maximizing quality of generic drugs, and enhancing efficiency in R&D innovations. More than one hundred foreign-developed drugs were approved for entry into the Chinese market in 2018.

The biotech industry was highlighted in three of the government's latest Five-Year Plans. An estimated $100 billion has already been invested in the life-sciences sector by central, provincial, and local governments to reach the Five-Year-Plan targets.

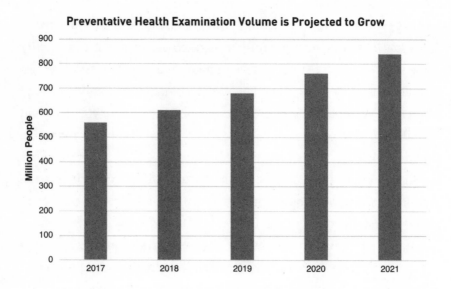

China has continued to break historical pharmaceutical sales records despite having significantly lower health care per capita expenditures compared to other major countries. China's pharmaceutical sales are projected to grow to $175 billion by 2022, according to health care information company IQVIA.[5] Per capita health spending remains low at $398, as compared to an average of over $6,500 in the world's top eight health care markets.

As average household income and urbanization rates have risen, Chinese citizens have greater access to health care knowledge and have a greater ability to pay for medical-related costs. In 2016, the government responded to growing health care concerns by launching the

"Healthy China 2030 Plan,"[6] which is a national initiative that promotes diet, exercise, and access to health care services.

By 2053, China will have 487 million senior citizens, making up 35 percent of the total population. The number of nursing homes in China is growing at a rate of 20.6 percent year-on-year to meet public demand; however, there currently is a shortage of medical care supplies for the elderly. For every 1,000 senior citizens, there are only 31.6 nursing home beds.

IT companies are leveraging China's robust internet infrastructure to increase efficiency and transparency in the health care R&D space. The medical device market has been one of the fastest growing health care segments in China, maintaining double-digit growth for over a decade. In 2019, the medical device market reached $96 billion, an increase of 22 percent compared to 2018. Over 70 percent of this growth is fueled by hospital procurements. The government's "Made in China 2025" initiative to improve industry efficiency, product quality, and brand reputation aims to further spur the development of domestic medical device manufacturers and increase the competitiveness of Chinese medical device brands.

As China's population becomes more health conscious, the demand for high quality preventative care also increases, providing a catalyst for private hospitals and facilities that offer health examinations, evaluations, and consulting services.

More than sixty of China's health care IPOs raised a record $16.3 billion in 2020. This total includes companies like COVID-19 vaccine developer CanSino Biologics Inc.[7]

In China's National Planning Guideline for the Healthcare Service System, the government aims to establish a nationally accessible digital health information database network that will integrate patient health profiles and medical records in electronic form. Guangdong province has already surpassed the adoption rate when Huizhou (a city within Guangdong) reached 91 percent of the city's population. As China's government continues to invest in internet-based health care services, utilization rates for those services are expected to grow.

Another aspect of the China Dream, beyond being healthy, is being happy. In the next chapter we'll look at the booming China leisure industry.

CHAPTER THIRTEEN
China at Leisure

A big component of the China Dream is domestic and international tourism. It wasn't that long ago that many rural people in China never left their home villages, and in some cases never encountered foreigners. A friend recalls that only two decades ago his American children were a major attraction for vacationing villagers in the Forbidden City in Beijing, and dozens of these villagers swarmed to take photos (always asking politely) of the toddlers, to show the folks back home.

But now, more and more of China's population can afford to take time off—and are being urged by their government to go forth and spend. In addition, the government has been spending to improve tourist attractions at home for both locals and international visitors.

A few years ago, the government decided to spend on developing Olympic sports, including swimming and diving, both for international prestige and to encourage the citizenry to exercise more. According to Bloomberg,[1] in the run-up to the 2020 Tokyo Summer Olympics (contested in 2021) China spent more than $1.5 billion on athlete training and facilities in 2019 and 2020 alone. The investment paid off with thirty-eight gold medals for Chinese athletes, just behind the leading U.S. total of thirty-nine. This was a Great Leap (pun intended) from twenty-six golds for China in 2016. They're going to spend a lot more ahead of the 2022 Winter Olympics in Beijing, and the authorities have announced plans to make sports a $775 billion a year industry by 2025, which would be a 70 percent increase from 2019.

All this effort is working. China is rapidly building up its leisure sector to encourage locals to spend more free time at home, and increasingly abroad, as well as welcoming more foreign tourists. I'm going to summarize findings from a recent CICC report:

Having an aging population and a declining number of children per family has contributed to the growth of the travel industry in other countries. Those retired at sixty-five have more leisure time, and the lower number of children per family means a lower cost burden for the younger generation of parents, both of which bode well for the travel industry.

The urbanization we looked at in chapter eight also appears to have had an impact on long-distance travel. Over the past twenty years, the number of long-distance trips by urban residents has increased by 13 percent, in contrast to 6 percent for rural residents. Urban residents made an average of 4.5 long-distance trips in 2017, versus only 2.3 trips for rural residents.

By comparison, Japan has an urbanization rate of 90 percent, and people there made an average of 5.3 long-distance trips in 2017.

On the back of China's economic development, a number of countries such as Canada, Japan, Thailand, the U.K., and Australia have relaxed their visa policies for Chinese citizens since 2017. Specific measures include simplifying the visa application process, shortening the processing time, raising the approval rate, and lengthening the visa validity period.

At the same time, the number of countries that allow Chinese citizens to visit without a visa or permit them to apply for one on arrival has grown. The number jumped from forty-three in 2010 to seventy-two in 2019.

It has also become easier to apply for visas in China's tier-2 cities. While in the past many countries had consulates only in tier-1 cities, the UK, Canada, France, Switzerland, Italy, and Germany, among others, have set up new visa application points in tier-2 cities such as Shenyang, Xi'an, Jinan, Wuhan, and Fuzhou to attract Chinese tourists.

Another factor that could make it easier for Chinese citizens to travel abroad is they no longer need to submit their household registers when applying for exit-entry documents. The application process has also been simplified: photo collection, fingerprint collection, application submission, face-to-face verification, and document payment can be done at the same time and at the same place.

A CICC report in 2019 found that the number of passport holders jumped from only 38 million in 2012 (about 3 percent of the total population) to 130 million at the end of 2017 (9.3 percent of the total population), rising at an annual rate of over 20 percent in recent years.

In developed economies, travel and related industries have generally grown twice as fast as GDP growth in the twenty years after GDP per capita reaches $9,000. The industry's growth rate then usually decelerates but stays on par with GDP growth after GDP per capita exceeds $30,000. In addition, spending on travel accounts for a rising percentage of total household expenditures after GDP per capita tops $9,000.

As we've seen, China's transportation infrastructure, such as roads, railways, and airports, has been rapidly improving. Transportation facilities in eastern parts of the country are already comparable to those in developed economies. China's public transport fares are inexpensive, with airfares declining steadily and railway fares rising at a modest rate. Meanwhile, the number of privately owned cars has risen steadily.

China's urban and rural residents make an average of 4.5 and 2.3 long-distance trips per year, respectively, again according to CICC. The average number of urban residents' long-distance trips per year has been growing twice as fast as the rural figure. Therefore, we believe that growth of the travel industry will receive a boost when China's urbanization rate exceeds 60 percent.

Chinese people's overseas travels will grow faster than their domestic trips, and the average distance of both domestic and overseas travels will grow. As China's living standard improves, we believe tourists will pay greater attention to comfort and experience rather than sightseeing alone. We think that an increasing percentage of tourists will choose to travel on their own rather than buying tour packages from travel agencies. In addition, we expect more and more tourists to drive their own cars and choose high-end accommodations with unique characteristics. Other forms of accommodation, such as homestays and short-term leases, are also on the rise. Tourist attractions with special features or cultural backgrounds will become increasingly popular.

Premium hotels and midrange to high-end hotels increasingly are the choice of travelers, especially those traveling abroad who have higher incomes and purchasing power and pay more attention to travel experience and comfort.

In the past, the hotel industry in China was characterized by a large proportion of guesthouses and five-star hotels, but a low proportion of other hotels. With the expansion of budget hotels in recent years, the proportion of hotels at different levels has become more balanced. Boutique hotels are increasingly being acquired by hotel chains. The share of chain hotels in China's hotel industry is only 38 percent, far below the 70 percent share in the U.S. The market share of the top three hotel groups in China is only 16 percent, also well below the 32 percent in the U.S. Still, Beijing and other major cities have enjoyed explosive growth in business-class hotels.

In addition to a more comfortable travel process, Chinese tourists also demand higher-quality travel content. In the past, sightseeing was the main purpose of tourists, and scenic spots were the main tourist attractions. Nowadays, the purpose of tourists is more diverse, with more attention paid to cultural experiences or leisure and fun.

As a result, museums, theme parks, film and television studios, and various resorts have become popular tourist attractions. The total number of long-distance trips by travelers from China during the 2018 National Day holiday reached 726 million, 13 percent of the full-year total. Tickets sold by cultural tourist attractions increased more than 36 percent year-on-year (versus 9 percent growth for total tourist attractions), and visitors to museums and art galleries increased more than 40 percent: The Louvre Museum in Paris and the Metropolitan Museum of Art in New York were among the ten most popular tourist attractions for China's overseas travelers in 2018.

Indeed, a friend reports that on a recent visit to Paris, the room in the Louvre that houses Leonardo da Vinci's *Mona Lisa*, in past years jammed wall-to-wall with Japanese tourists, was now jammed wall-to-wall with tourists from China.

Traditional popular tourist attractions have also upgraded to enhance the cultural experience of visitors. At the same time, travel agencies such as China International Travel Service have launched cultural theme tours to attract tourists. Theme parks are springing up in China: Amusement parks (i.e., Disneyland) and film and television studios (i.e., Wanda Studios and Hengdian World Studios) have emerged as new popular tourist attractions.

According to infrastructure firm AECOM, 156 city-level theme parks are operating in China with more than seventy under construction. The total attendance of theme parks in China increased 20 percent to 190 million in 2018. AECOM expects the total attendance of theme parks in China to reach 230 million in 2021, exceeding that in the U.S. and making China the world's largest theme park market.[2]

The aggregate expenditures of outbound China tourists remain the largest around the globe, and shopping is the biggest category of overseas spending by these tourists, who spent about $255 billion abroad in 2019,[3] almost double that of second-ranked U.S. tourists.

China's recently discovered penchant for travel is right in line with the experience of other nations with burgeoning middle classes. As passengers in China switch from low-speed to high-speed modes of transport amid a quickening pace of life and a continuous decline in air fares, high-speed rail and air transport companies are gaining market share in China. Before the emergence of high-speed rail in 2008, the proportion of rail transport among China's overall passenger turnover declined steadily to 33 percent in 2008 from 63 percent in 1978.

Since China launched its first high-speed railway in 2008, high-speed rail passenger traffic has increased by 84 percent, and the proportion of rail transport among China's overall passenger turnover reached 41 percent in 2018. The proportion of air transport in China's overall passenger turnover has been rising before and after the emergence of high-speed rail, to 31 percent from 10 percent over the past thirty years. Even excluding international routes, the proportion of air transport in domestic passenger turnover increased to 23 percent in 2017 from 6 percent in 2007.

Developed countries such as the U.S., Japan, the U.K., France, and Germany have experienced the transition from economical transport modes (bus, ordinary rail) to time-sensitive transport modes (air, express rail) as household incomes rise. From 1980 to 2000, the proportion of air transport in the U.S.'s overall passenger turnover increased rapidly to 13 percent from 4 percent, while that of light-rail and ordinary rail transport declined; since 2000, the proportion of air transport has increased further, to 17 percent.

Based on foreign countries' historical data and the Chinese government's statistical data, overseas travel should grow faster than domestic travel, with gradually longer average distances for both overseas and domestic travel. The number of overseas trips by Chinese travelers increased rapidly by 35 times during the past 25 years, faster than the 10 times increase in the number of domestic trips. The number of overseas trips by Chinese travelers increased to 160 million in 2018 from 5 million in 1994, while the number of domestic trips increased to 5.1 billion from 500 million. About 170 million Chinese citizens traveled internationally in 2019 (before COVID).[4]

Historically, Hong Kong, Macau, and Taiwan have been the destinations for a vast majority of overseas travelers from mainland China. However, over the past ten years, overseas travel from mainland China to these locations grew at a slower pace than the travel to other regions, with Thailand and Japan becoming the new mainstream destinations. As China's incremental overseas travel demand mainly comes from its tier-2 and tier-3 cities, we believe Asian countries and regions will remain the key destinations for China's overseas travelers for some time, but travel to farther destinations will likely enjoy higher growth in the future.

In addition to travel, people in China are spending more on other leisure pursuits, especially entertainment.

A major company in this sector is Bilibili, an innovative and growing online entertainment platform in China. Bilibili is akin to YouTube in the U.S., but offers a wider variety of content, including games and comics. Since its U.S. IPO in 2018, the company's stock has returned nearly 200 percent. In July 2020, I spoke with a number of Bilibili executives to find out more about the company's growth, challenges, and U.S. listing.[5] Their thoughts are condensed below:

"Bilibili's mission is to enrich the everyday life of young generations in China. A substantial portion of Bilibili users are Generation Z—individuals born from 1990 to 2009 in China. We started as a content community inspired by anime, comics, and games, or ACG. Our website was first launched in 2009 as a personal interest site by a group of college friends who enjoyed anime. At the time, our founder Yi Xu was 20 years old. Since the inception of our company, Mr. Xu has been an opinion leader in our communities and led the prosperity of our community culture among users.

"In 2011, our current Chairman and CEO Rui Chen, a serious anime fan, met Yi Xu and funded our first round of financing as an angel investor. Mr. Chen is a serial entrepreneur. He started his career at Kingsoft (HK: 3888), founded Beike Internet Security Co., Ltd., then joined Cheetah Mobile (NYSE: CMCM) as a co-founder, and officially joined Bilibili after Cheetah Mobile listed on the New York Stock Exchange. We have evolved into a full-spectrum online entertainment world covering a wide array of genres and media formats, including videos, live broadcasting, and mobile games.

"We attract private equity investors because of the following three reasons: our unique content, our close-knit community environment, and our core users. We have been in a unique position since the first day we launched Bilibili. We have a very healthy, user-generated content ecosystem where talented creators produce high-quality content, which we call professional user-generated content (PUGC). Our expanding content library and our enthusiastic community keep attracting new users and motivating creators.

"We also have an incredibly engaged community that encourages users to interact with our distinctly innovative and interactive features. For example, we pioneered the bullet chat feature, a live commenting function that has transformed the viewing experience. This signature feature fosters a highly interactive and enjoyable viewing experience and allows our users to benefit from strong emotional bonds with other users who share similar aspirations and interests. We are an iconic brand amongst Chinese youth, the 'golden cohort' for the future entertainment market. By capturing this group of users, we hope to capture the future of the online entertainment market.

"Bilibili's premium membership runs on a subscription model, which allows premium members to enjoy exclusive content or view licensed content as well as original content in advance. As of March 31, 2020, we had 10.9 million valid premium members. Our premium member count has increased by 127% since March 31, 2019. Bilibili's advertising business contributed RMB 214 million in the first quarter of 2020, a 90.5% increase compared to the same period last year. During the first quarter, coinciding with COVID-19, our advertising revenue experienced steady growth.

"We are increasingly recognized as the go-to platform to communicate with young generations. In the future, our growing community and increased brand equity will make Bilibili a leading platform for advertisers. Live broadcasting is a natural extension of our video platform. Game, music, dancing, and drawing shows have accounted for a substantial majority of the content offered on our live broadcasting program in 2019. We have also started several initiatives to expand our live broadcasting content, such as live streaming e-sports games, to cater to our game lover users, including top-level matches in League of Legends and the Overwatch League Championships. In December 2019, we entered into a letter of intent to purchase the three-year license for live broadcasting the League of Legends World Championship in China starting from 2020, the crown jewel of the e-sports world. Our investment in live-broadcasting IP continues to fuel our user growth and attract more live-broadcasting hosts. We are seeing more talent agencies and individuals turn to Bilibili to expand their influence through our platform." (Bilibili recently linked with Sony in a marketing agreement.)

Increasing international travel by people, a key part of the China Dream, is almost always followed by increasing international trade, and not just for items tourists might see abroad. Trade is a huge part of the China Dream. We'll look at that next.

CHAPTER FOURTEEN
Trade

As the realization of the China Dream continues to improve living standards at home, much is made of trade tensions between China and its trading partners.

The last U.S. administration made trade with China a central issue, now being pursued by the Biden administration. Negotiations have come and gone, and punitive tariffs have been applied on various China-made goods (and in retaliation by China on American goods) from time to time. Thankfully, a truce was reached in January 2020 and the new administration is developing a new strategy.

Trade is one of the issues I follow most closely, because it's so important to both building bridges between countries and helping both Chinese and Americans to realize their dreams. Even though I run an investment firm, I spend a lot of time with experts like Henry Kissinger and others you'll meet soon on this issue.

A report by the U.S. Chamber of Commerce and the Rhodium Group in February 2021 lays out the huge stakes. "In the trade channel, if 25% tariffs were expanded to cover all two-way trade, the U.S. would forgo $190 billion in GDP annually by 2025. The stakes are even higher when accounting for how lost U.S. market access in China today creates revenue and job losses, lost economies of scale, smaller research and development (R&D) budgets, and diminished competitiveness.

"In the investment channel, if decoupling leads to the sale of half of the U.S. foreign direct investment (FDI) stock in China, U.S. investors would lose $25 billion per year in capital gains, and models point to one-time GDP losses of up to $500 billion. Reduced FDI from China to the U.S. would add to the costs and—by flowing elsewhere instead—likely benefit U.S. competitors.

"In people flows, the COVID-19 pandemic has demonstrated the economic impact from lost tourism from China and education spending. If future flows are reduced by half from their pre-COVID levels, the U.S. would lose between $15 billion and $30 billion per year in services and exports.

"In idea flows, decoupling would undermine U.S. productivity and innovation, but quantification in this regard is difficult. U.S. business R&D at home to support operations in China would fall and companies from other countries would reduce R&D spending related to their China ambitions in the U.S. The longer-term implications could include supply chain diversion away from U.S. players, less attraction for venture capital investment in U.S. innovation, and global innovation competition as other nations try to fill the gap."

While the trade war taught us that we are a connected global economy, the coronavirus pandemic shows that we are a global community. At a time when international unity is more necessary than ever, we believe the desire for increased cooperation will be the prevailing sentiment as the world reopens—even if headlines do not always appear that way. This was our KraneShares assessment in mid-2020 and it still holds true.[1]

As we've seen, there was a tremendous amount of positive momentum generated from the signing of the Phase One trade agreement in 2020. While the coronavirus pandemic diverted attention away from these accomplishments, we believe it is essential to focus on strengthening the win-win aspects of the relationship between the U.S. and China for the following reasons:[2]

1. A cooperative relationship between the world's two largest economies is more important now than ever.

   While the common perception is that U.S.–China relations were only strained further due to coronavirus, China and the U.S. supported each other at the government, business, and individual level throughout the pandemic. As both countries have the highest numbers of clinical trials currently in motion, a cooperative relationship would ensure that the vaccine reaches the world's population as efficiently as possible.

2. U.S. companies continue to look to China's consumer market for growth.

   American companies are increasingly relying on the China consumer as a key source of revenue growth. In 2017, the most recent year for which there is official data, U.S. multinationals generated revenue of approximately $376 billion in China.[3] Despite rhetoric from U.S. leaders, U.S. companies have found that the China consumer nonetheless continues to appreciate American brands and takes "made in the USA" as a sign of quality.

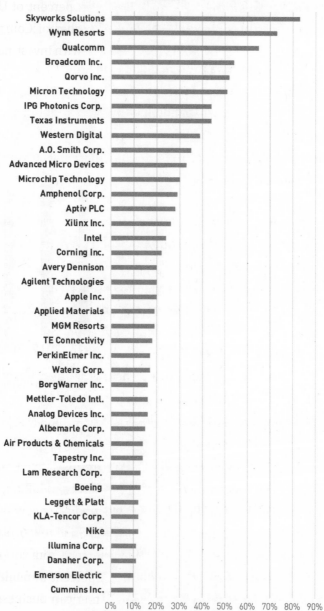

S&P 500 Members With 10%+ Revenue Exposure to China

Data from Goldman Sachs as of July 2018. Revenue figures for Advanced Micro Devices, Apple, and Ilumina Inc. include revenue from Taiwan; all other figures refer to revenue from Mainland China only.

Paradoxically, American investment in China has remained steady through the trade war. Thirty-six percent of U.S. businesses surveyed by the American Chamber of Commerce in China said that they would move forward with investment plans regardless of guidance from Washington.

US FDI in China

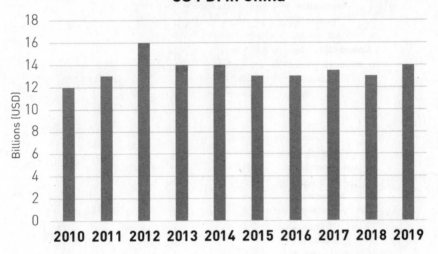

Data from Rhodium Group.

3. Trade with China supports more than 1.1 million U.S. jobs.

Under the Phase One trade agreement, signed by the two governments in January 2020, China promised to increase agricultural purchases from the U.S. by nearly $40 billion, offering significant relief for farmers, many of whom are now seeing the impact from the coronavirus pandemic. Goods exports to China grew at an average annual rate of 6.2 percent from 2009 to 2018, while services exports grew at a 15.2 percent annualized rate from 2008 to 2017. In recent years, American businesses have profited greatly from trading with China. However, due to the

Jobs Supported By Exports To China By State

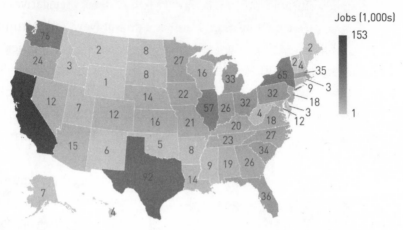

Data from US-China Business Council, The Trade Partnership (Washington, DC).
Numbers rounded to the nearest thousand.

recent trade war, goods exports to China contracted for the first time in a decade, falling by 7.4 percent from 2017 to 2018.

We believe carrying out the Phase One trade deal is in our best interest as well as China's. The Phase One trade deal involved, among other provisions, a commitment by China to respect intellectual property rights and increase its purchases of U.S. goods. Thanks to China's compliance with the terms of the agreement, China surpassed Canada and Mexico to become the U.S.'s largest trade partner in April 2020.

4. The trade war hurt U.S. stocks.

Trade headlines tend to ripple through markets and dampen business confidence all over the world. U.S. equity markets surged once the U.S. and China signed a trade deal in

January 2020. Equity markets on both sides of the Pacific have consistently contracted with every trade tweet or negative communication. The Federal Reserve Bank of New York estimates that every significant announcement of new trade restrictions was followed by an average 2.9 percent drop in the stock price of affected companies within five days of the announcement. According to the NY Fed, announcements of trade restrictions have lowered the market capitalization of U.S.-listed firms by $1.7 trillion so far.

Fortunately, the U.S. and China have been communicative on trade, and the Phase One deal remains in effect. State-owned firms purchased over one million tons of soybeans in only two weeks in May 2020, some of which are scheduled for future delivery.[4] The purchases came after China had already begun to increase purchases of other agricultural products such as wheat and sorghum since the Phase One agreement was signed.

5. U.S. investors cannot ignore China's recovery.

We believe there are currently multiple tailwinds for growth in Chinese stocks. These include an economy that has been swiftly recovering from the pandemic, valuations that may rise thanks to new STAR market and Hong Kong listings, significant recent steps to further open mainland markets that are being applauded by the global investor community, and a thriving domestic market that has survived the pandemic.

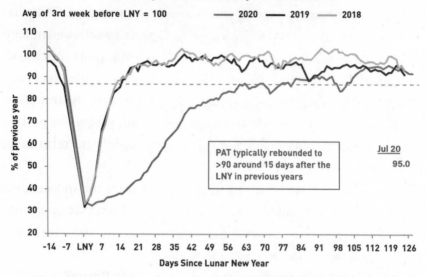

LNY: Lunar New Year. The production activity tracker (PAT) is an index tracking the level of industrial output across companies surveyed by CICC throughout China. The index level is expressed as a percentage of the level recorded on the same calendar day the year before (2019). Source: CICC Research.

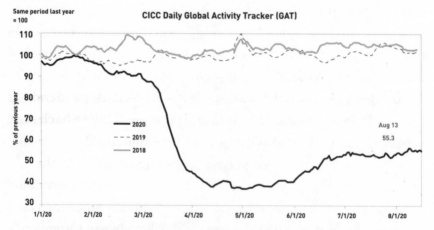

The global activity tracker (GAT) is an index tracking the level of industrial output across companies surveyed by CICC throughout the world. The index level is expressed as a percentage of the level recorded on the same calendar day the year before (2019). Source: CICC Research.

China has the advantage of having been the first country to experience the pandemic and therefore is likely to recover first. China has mostly restarted its vast production engine as well as allowed numerous offline businesses to reopen, including restaurants, brick-and-mortar retail, and movie theaters. With offline businesses reopened in most provinces, China already has a head start over the rest of the world. As my colleague Brendan Ahern has said, we believe participating in this recovery in demand may yield significant returns for global investors.[5]

In late 2020, I spoke with David Metzner from the independent research firm ACG Analytics about what to expect from the new administration's approach to China and Chinese companies, and have reproduced our conversation here:[6]

What are your views on Biden's approach to China?

"Based upon what we know of Biden's cabinet appointees, including Tony Blinken for secretary of state, Jake Sullivan for national security advisor, and Janet Yellen for treasury secretary, we believe that Biden's approach to China will be based more on engagement and reliant upon international coalition building. His approach will still address technology and supply chains but will also shift focus toward environmental issues, areas in which international support are effective."

Biden's priority will be tackling the COVID-19 pandemic as cases rise. Does this mean that China policy will take a back seat, or will Biden be able to tackle both at the same time?

"Domestic policy is likely to dominate foreign policy in the first one to two years of the Biden presidency. However, the administration is capable of addressing several matters at once and China's increased global diplomatic and military presence will likely demand attention."

The U.S. Chamber of Commerce had no voice in the previous White House after speaking out against tariffs. Do you see them

having a louder voice in the Biden administration? Will U.S. business interests in China have a voice?

"Yes, we do see corporate interests as having more influence under the Biden administration. Policymaking will be the result of a deliberate and slow interagency process at the White House, taking all viewpoints into account."

Will a removal of or reduction in trade tariffs be a feature of Biden's China policy?

"Because of his limited ability to address China immediately, we believe that he will enact a full-scale review of tariff and trade policies left over from the previous administration and freeze any major decision-making until the review is complete. This review is likely to cover executive orders as well as existing tariffs. Ultimately, we do believe that Biden will remove or lower tariffs on China, just not immediately. China could approach the Biden administration to revise the Phase One trade agreement, which he is likely to agree to if it includes significant concessions in other areas."

Trade is certainly an issue both the U.S. and China will have to navigate carefully. But China's economy is in a different place today from where it was a decade ago. Today, services have surpassed manufacturing as the largest contributor to China's economy, representing over 50 percent of GDP, while manufacturing only represents 40 percent.[7]

While segments of China's economy have been adversely affected by trade wars, exports are a smaller part of China's GDP than they are frequently portrayed. In reality, exports represent less than 20 percent of China's total GDP, and exports to the U.S. are only 4 percent of China's total GDP. Internet-based companies such as Tencent, Alibaba, Baidu, Trip.com, and Weibo are all focused on the China domestic market and have limited exposure to global trade policy. These companies are currently growing revenue at a much faster rate than their U.S. equivalents.

China has undergone a massive shift in recent years, which has transformed its economy. While trade tension-fueled volatility can be discouraging, we believe investors who are interested in China may benefit from taking a long-term view, looking beyond the headlines. Focusing too much on the exports and manufacturing that defined China's old economy can detract from real opportunities occurring right now in China's services sector and domestic market.

The Economist recently ran a map, based on IMF data, that showed the remarkable swing from the U.S. to China as the major trading partner among many countries, since 2001 (see page 216).[8] As we've seen with the Belt and Road Initiative, trade is a cornerstone of China's foreign policy all over the world, and especially with the U.S.

Let's take a deep dive into the issues of trade and the intertwined U.S. and China economies.

According to the United States Department of Agriculture (USDA), as of the end of 2016, China was the largest importer of U.S. agricultural products. Last year, China was responsible for buying $21.4 billion, or over 15.9 percent, of the United States' total $134.9 billion agriculture exports.

As incomes rise in China, the demand for U.S. agriculture products has also grown due to the increasingly discerning tastes and health-conscious attitude of China's urban middle class. When U.S.-based Costco Wholesale Corporation established a storefront on Alibaba's T-mall, a virtual mall, days before Singles' Day 2014, the world's largest online shopping holiday, they sold over three tons of nuts and one ton of dried cranberries to China consumers in a matter of days.

As previously mentioned, a Chinese company, Shuanghui International Holdings Ltd, bought Smithfield Foods, the largest U.S. pork processor. Shuanghui sells Smithfield pork through Alibaba under the Shuanghui brand with an American flag displayed prominently on the label.[9]

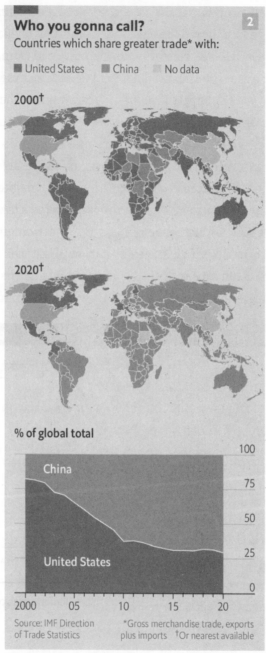

Who you gonna call?

Countries which share greater trade* with:

■ United States ■ China ■ No data

2000†

2020†

% of global total

China

United States

Source: IMF Direction of Trade Statistics

*Gross merchandise trade, exports plus imports †Or nearest available

The Economist

That American flag packaging tells Chinese consumers that the food comes from the United States. It is an indication of quality and reliability. The USDA has established a large presence in China to help U.S. farmers navigate local regulations and sell their products in China.

As mentioned in chapter four, beyond agriculture, many U.S. businesses are profiting from the Chinese consumer. China's urban middle class increasingly has a taste for Western goods that goes beyond agricultural products. America's auto industry, led by General Motors, is also thriving in China. China has been GM's largest retail market for the past five years. In 2019, GM and its joint ventures delivered a record 3,870,587 vehicles in China. GM has achieved this success through eleven joint ventures and two wholly owned foreign enterprises as well as more than 58,000 employees in China. GM is also selling cars online. During Singles' Day 2016, GM sold four thousand Chevy Cruzes through Alibaba.

Company	Apple		Nike		Starbucks		Under Armour	
Fiscal Year	2020	2011	2020	2011	2020	2011	2020	2011
% of Revenue from Greater China or Asia Pacific Region	14.7%	11.7%	18.8%	9.9%	11.0%	4.7%	14.0%	N/A
Dollar Amount of Revenue from the Region	$40.3B	$12.7B	$6.7B	$2.1B	$2.6B	$522 mm	$628 mm	N/A
Specific Region	Greater China		Greater China		Greater China		Asia Pacific	

Data from Company Annual Reports and Bloomberg as of 12/31/2020.

U.S. brands can achieve increased sales in China through partnerships with domestic Chinese companies. There are a number of high-profile partnerships that highlight the popularity of this model.

On June 20, 2016, Walmart announced it was acquiring approximately 5 percent of JD.com, Alibaba's chief rival. The strategic alliance was formed to help Walmart access additional consumers across China through a powerful combination of ecommerce and retail. In August 2014, Priceline invested $500 million in Ctrip through convertible bonds. Priceline's agreement enables it to share inventory and thereby capture outbound traffic from China.

While Tesla sold nearly $3 billion worth of cars in China in 2020, it sold a 5 percent share to Tencent to further assist in automotive sales. According to a report from CNBC,[10] Tencent could help Tesla sell—and build—cars in China, the world's largest auto market, while Tesla got a leg up in the self-driving car market in China; currently China partners provide U.S. companies with strategic guidance for navigating local rules, regulations, and cultural tastes. Partnering with Chinese technology companies can bring access to massive platforms for reaching new customers that would otherwise be unattainable. Tesla's partnership with Tencent gives the firm access to Tencent's 800 million monthly users. Even for a successful company like Tesla, building an audience of 800 million would likely be impossible.

Even with all these examples of U.S. businesses thriving in China, the topic of trade imbalance is still a point of contention. We believe too much emphasis on the perceived one-sided nature of the relationship ignores both the growing demand for U.S. goods and services among Chinese consumers and a core principle of trade. When an emerging market country and a developed market country trade with one another, the developed market has more money to buy more goods from the emerging market. This imbalance is the primary reason a trade deficit exists between the United States and China.

Stepping back, U.S. exports to China have been on the rise over the past several decades. In 1990, the U.S. exported $5 billion worth of goods to China, by 2000 that number grew to $16 billion, and by 2010 it reached $91 billion. Last year the U.S. topped $115 billion worth of goods exported to China. While this number is much lower than the amount we imported from China ($462 billion), it still shows healthy growth, and a major opportunity for U.S. exporters.

Chances are that, despite trade tensions, U.S. exports to China will continue to accelerate in the years to come. The wage gap has been narrowing, especially among China's urban middle class. This segment of China's population increasingly has a taste for American and Western goods. Whether you are an unexpected beneficiary of this trend, like the American farmer, or a global corporation, like GM and Costco, there are two key points to remember when selling U.S. products in China:

1. It helps to find a local partner.
2. The China consumer prefers to shop online.

According to the U.S. Census Bureau, the United States imports more cars from Canada[11] than from any other country in the world. Considering this statistic, you would assume that Canadian car brands like Intermeccanica and Campagna would be household names in the U.S., but they are not. The U.S. Census Bureau defines imports as "all goods physically brought into the United States"; therefore, in reality, the bulk of the Canadian cars referenced in this statistic are Fords, Chevys, and Lincolns assembled in Canadian plants and shipped back to the US. Even though the revenues of these cars go to the Detroit-based companies and their shareholders, the U.S. Census Bureau still considers them Canadian. In fact, this extends to many other U.S. products that are manufactured in other countries. Almost 50 percent of the S&P 500's revenues are derived from abroad, meaning that the wealth of every American investor is dependent on U.S. companies' ability to participate in international trade.

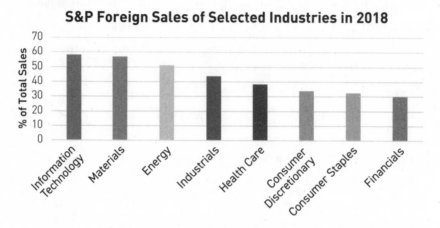

S&P Foreign Sales of Selected Industries in 2018

Data from "S&P 500 2018: Global Sales" as of 12/31/2018.

Data from the U.S. Census Bureau shows that the U.S. trade deficit with China was $311 billion in 2020; however, this statistic does not recognize profits of U.S. products manufactured locally in China. Therefore, a large portion of U.S. trade with China is not reflected in the trade deficit metric. For example, products like Apple's iPhone, which are assembled in China and brought back for sale in the U.S., contribute to the U.S.–China trade deficit, as they are considered Chinese goods despite the revenues flowing to Apple in Cupertino, CA.

Over the past decade, U.S. direct investment in China has increased steadily, nearly doubling from $54 billion in 2009 to $107 billion in 2017. This is true across a wide range of sectors and industries. For example, Ford and its China joint-venture partner, Chang'an Ford Mazda Automobile, built two plants in China from 2012 to 2014 for a total investment of over $800 million.

Tyson Foods also established three poultry processing operations in China from 2001 to 2013 with over 4,300 employees, and in 2016, Wynn Resorts opened a new $4.2 billion resort in Macau. These are just a few examples of rising U.S. investment in China, and even more investments are happening, such as Tesla's construction of a $2 billion plant in Shanghai capable of rivaling its facility in California.

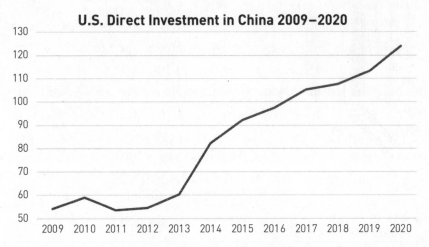

U.S. Direct Investment in China 2009–2020

Data from US Department of Commerce Bureau of Economic Analysis as of 12/31/2020.

Increased investment in China has also led to more revenues for American companies. For example, Apple had net sales of $40.5 billion in China for the nine-month period ending in June 2018, about a 16 percent increase year to date, and Nike's revenues in China have increased from $635 million in 2013 to $1.34 billion in 2018, an increase of 110 percent in just five years. Moreover, U.S. companies have benefited from the export of services to China, where the U.S. ran a trade surplus of $38.4 billion in 2017.

When all these factors are added to conduct a deeper trade analysis, the U.S.–China trade deficit is much lower than reported. One study published in March 2017 used newly available data from the World Input-Output Database (WIOD) to show that the U.S.–China trade deficit for goods and services in 2014 was around $100 billion lower than the U.S. Census Bureau's official estimate. Also, when you limit trade to services, the U.S. has actually run a steady surplus with China since trade between the two nations was first made possible under Nixon.

With U.S. companies benefiting greatly from trade with China, we believe it is unlikely that trade tensions will progress to the more extreme scenarios. Increasing the size of tariffs with China over a prolonged period of time could have a substantial impact on U.S. and global economic growth. General Electric estimated that new tariffs on its imports from China could raise its costs by $300 million to $400 million overall, and Whirlpool, an American appliance giant, now expects to pay $350 million more for raw materials due to tariffs.

Former Ford CEO James Hackett recently described the effect of tariffs on his company, stating, "the metals tariffs took about $1 billion in profit from us . . . The irony of which is we source most of that in the U.S. today anyway. If it goes on any longer, it will do more damage." Over the past couple of years, U.S. companies filed nearly three thousand comments with the U.S. Trade Representative's Office opposing more tariffs.

The Biden administration is sensitive to the performance of the U.S. stock market, and we believe that they will not push tariffs so far that they have a prolonged negative impact on U.S. companies.

In his address to my colleagues and me, mentioned earlier, Dr. Kissinger[12] shared that he was confident the current trade dispute will be resolved eventually because resolution is in the best interests of both the U.S. and China. Beijing and Washington need a resolution of the conflict. The Phase One agreement was just a start. Both leaders face economic and political pressures, which currently compel each side to reach a solution. China has already signaled a willingness to address the U.S.'s main concerns.

For four decades, China's leaders have promised their people increasing prosperity. As a result, China will compromise on trade issues with the U.S. if it perceives that failing to do so will hurt the economy.

In addition, Kissinger noted that a trade resolution is only a near-term solution. The issues surrounding U.S.–China relations in both trade and other areas will persist for a very long time.

The U.S. needs to be cognizant of these realities as it negotiates with China. Kissinger said he would not have taken the approach Washington has taken with China. However, Kissinger also noted that Washington's approach has achieved a lot more in a shorter period of time than traditional diplomatic approaches would have accomplished.

Kissinger added that the trade issues with China needed to be confronted at some point. Challenging China while it is still ascending makes a lot more sense than waiting until it has accreted a lot more power, at which point economic issues could turn into security issues.

The January 2020 resolution of Phase One of the trade negotiations came as welcome news for markets. The U.S. agreed to cut tariffs by half in exchange for actionable promises from China on intellectual property, joint ventures, and increasing agricultural purchases. However, there remains work to be done to build a mutually beneficial future relationship between the U.S. and China. Kissinger is more concerned about the long-term implications and precedents that may be set for future conflict and negotiations, and how the two sides can create a long-term sustainable relationship.

In June 2021 I had the honor of talking to former U.S. ambassador to China Max Baucus and former U.S. ambassador to Singapore David Adelman, who is now a KraneShares managing director and our general counsel. Here's what they had to say:[13]

Ambassador Baucus described the current U.S. policy toward China as driven by domestic politics rather than rational geopolitical considerations. Baucus believes we can expect the Biden administration to strike a more conciliatory tone when compared to the Trump administration's more confrontational approach. However, he said the Biden administration will continue to take a firm line with the country that is home to the world's second-largest economy.

Baucus and Adelman entered the foreign service at a time when American foreign policy was turning toward the Asia-Pacific region after having been concentrated on the Middle East for the first decade of the twenty-first century. According to Baucus, Obama's "Pivot to Asia" came with the startling revelation that China could be America's equal. Regarding the current foreign policy situation, Baucus noted that perhaps tension between a rising power and an incumbent power is inevitable.

Baucus characterized the Obama administration's approach to China as centered on engagement with China and the development of partnerships in the Asia-Pacific region. Baucus supported President Obama's signature multilateral trade agreement, the Trans-Pacific Partnership (TPP), which did not include China but included some of the other large economies in Asia, such as Japan, Vietnam, and Singapore. Baucus thinks the past administration's decision to abandon the agreement set the U.S. back in its relations with China's Asian neighbors. Meanwhile, he noted that China has stepped up its engagement with the international community, especially the developing world, through the Belt and Road Initiative, Asian Infrastructure Investment Bank (AIIB), and the Regional Comprehensive Economic Partnership (RCEP). He noted that U.S. ally Australia participates in both the AIIB and RCEP.

The challenges presented by U.S. policies force a choice for countries in Asia between the U.S. and China. With the growing economic strength of China, many Asian countries that have always been U.S. allies may nonetheless find themselves in a difficult position, having to choose between trade with China and security engagement with the U.S.

Ambassador Adelman asked Baucus whether the Biden administration will revive some elements of the Obama administration's policy of engagement with China. Baucus responded that while he could not say for certain, his feeling is that due to the current state of U.S. politics and the critical domestic issues facing President Biden, warming relations with China would not happen quickly but he remained optimistic. He said a comprehensive reassessment of the China relationship is likely on hold for the time being because of the Biden administration's focus on the pandemic and U.S. infrastructure needs.

Baucus's greatest concern regarding the U.S.–China relationship is a lack of communication between Washington and Beijing. He noted that both the U.S. and China are going to great lengths to secure their supply chains to be less dependent on global trade for specific products. He views such efforts as positive as they reduce the risk of supply shocks that can lead to conflict. However, he urged the U.S. to stop viewing China's efforts at securing its own supply chain with suspicion, saying that China is acting rationally. I couldn't agree more.

Baucus emphasized his concern about a breakdown in lines of communication between the two countries. This concern was the same as that expressed by former U.S. secretary of state Kissinger in our conversation with him in 2018. Baucus said there was much more interaction between the U.S. and China during his time as ambassador, and he hopes that level of interaction will return. Nonetheless, Baucus is "cautiously optimistic" that relations between the world's two powers may improve.

Regarding existing tariffs, investment restrictions, and the U.S. Holding Foreign Companies Accountable Act (HFCA), Baucus said there are currently too many protective policies in place, which will eventually begin to damage the U.S. economy. Having served in the U.S. Senate with President Biden for decades, he thinks the Biden administration will recognize that some of these policies are not in America's best interests and there will likely be some easing of restrictions.

Baucus outlined potential areas of cooperation between the U.S. and China in the short and long term. According to both former diplomats, the two powers are most likely to cooperate on combating climate change. Baucus said that China will try to lead the world on climate change. However, he noted that China has considerable ground to cover to achieve its goal of carbon neutrality by 2060.

Baucus said that when the U.S. left the Paris Agreement on climate change, China took the opportunity to fill the void. Now that President Biden has returned the U.S. to the agreement, the two countries will be inclined to work together. Baucus is also upbeat about the further integration of the two countries' financial services industries. After being permitted to do so for the first time in 2019, JPMorgan and Goldman Sachs, among other large U.S. banks and brokerage houses, will set up deeper presences in China. Baucus said American financial institutions cannot pass up the China opportunity. Likewise, Baucus is pleased by China's progress in opening its capital markets to foreign investment. He was the U.S. ambassador in China when the Shanghai-Hong Kong Stock Connect program was established and acknowledged its benefit to China's capital markets.

Baucus remains close with leaders in both Beijing and Washington and thinks they will look for common ground. He acknowledges that the Biden administration will leave some previous policies in place in the near term but expects there to be loosening of restrictions after a close review of the cost of certain policies to the U.S.

Successful diplomacy depends upon understanding each other's needs and talking through and analyzing problems together. By doing so, each side has a basic understanding of how the other side will see a situation when difficulties arise. This understanding tends to minimize the number of conflicts and their severity. It also creates a path for resolving conflicts.

"On a recent visit to China, I met with a wide variety of financial institutions to discuss their views on the current economic relationship between the United States and China," shared my colleague Brendan Ahern, summing up where we are and where we're going.[14] "Interestingly, their sentiment toward the U.S. was still extremely positive. Many compared our countries to a married couple currently having a disagreement. No one doubted the fundamental value of the relationship, but they were uneasy about the abrupt change in U.S. negotiation tactics. The market volatility caused by trade tensions stems from domestic Chinese investors who take their leader's words as definitive policy and apply the same logic to the U.S. president. Evidently, misconceptions work both ways. The Chinese hold them regarding us, too."

We believe China's economy is more resilient than 2019 or 2020 headlines portrayed. Three macro trends suggest that tariffs will have a relatively muted long-term impact on economic fundamentals in China: 1) Economic growth is increasingly fueled by demand from domestic consumers, 2) Chinese policymakers began weaning the economy off foreign demand through monetary policy long before any talk of tariffs, and 3) Chinese firms are likely to maintain, or even augment, their present competitive advantages should protectionism persist.

China's economic ministers have long viewed the domestic consumer as the key to sustainable economic growth. In recent years this has been most evident in China's tight monetary policy implemented through credit reduction. China has actively curtailed the long-standing practice of large Chinese conglomerates issuing local debt, then using it to buy predominantly U.S. dollar–denominated foreign assets. This practice drove down the value of the renminbi (RMB) and the purchasing power of the Chinese consumer. In response, the government implemented capital controls to slow down these outflows. Additionally, the government has initiated a de-leveraging campaign, mostly targeting so-called "shadow banking," mentioned in chapter five.

As a result of these policies, the RMB has remained stable enough to keep the Chinese consumer consistently empowered and optimistic. While trade war pressure on the RMB could potentially jeopardize these tightening policies, the People's Bank of China is still in a good position to find the right balance between quantitative easing and reform.

In a recent research report, CICC noted that some easing will be necessary to offset trade pressures, though, in the best-case scenario, it will be accompanied by policy reforms to avoid a permanent slide in the currency and a regression toward the "old" Chinese economy. The rate of easing then accelerated in response to the coronavirus outbreak.

In 2012, the European Central Bank (ECB) began a similar aggressive quantitative easing program in response to the debt crisis. However, unlike China, whose strong central government can easily implement policy, the ECB was unable to fully back up the program with cohesive austerity policies across all its member states.

Furthermore, China is still the single largest owner of U.S. treasuries, which makes a full-fledged currency war unlikely. Countries such as Turkey, Argentina, and Brazil have been negatively impacted by a rising dollar because they run current account deficits with dollar-denominated debt. China is in the opposite position because it benefits from appreciation in its substantial U.S. dollar holdings. Additionally, most credit growth in China comes from corporations and not from the central government. Thus, China policymakers are well positioned to ensure that companies posing systematic risks are provided support without impacting the government's credit profile.

Finally, the competitive advantages of China firms, even those whose revenues are heavily export driven, are likely to survive further protectionism. China firms usually account for the most labor-intensive segments of supply chains headed to the U.S. and other developed countries. It is unlikely that any level of protectionism will cut out this competitive advantage in auto manufacturing and many other similarly export-dependent industries.

Retaliatory tariffs likely handed those China firms that see intense competition from multinationals a significant price advantage in China. This has been especially the case for local players in software, automobiles, medical equipment, and agriculture.

Throughout 2019, China equities were severely undervalued compared to their U.S. counterparts. This deep undervaluation is partially due to individual investors reacting to headlines coming out of the United States. Unlike in the U.S., where institutional investors dominate the market, retail investors own the vast majority of the Chinese mainland market. Across the board, individuals are more reactive to sentiment than institutions. Individual investors in China are accustomed to a political environment in which their president's words are taken as policy. However, ownership of China's stock market is steadily being institutionalized.

This undervaluation occurred just as leading global index provider MSCI completed the second phase in their ongoing inclusion of mainland stocks in their emerging markets index, which is tracked by $1.9 trillion worth of actively and passively managed assets. Also, in 2019, foreign asset managers were permitted, for the first time, to launch mutual funds and hedge funds in China without a local partner.

Tariffs on exports from China to the United States do not negate the strong fundamentals of China stocks and the new Chinese economy. As import tariffs are, first and foremost, a bargaining chip, it is likely that the U.S. will ease the pressure once underlying disputes are resolved. At that point, the marriage between the world's two largest economies can return to normal, hopefully without friction or long-term impact, creating value for people on both sides of the Pacific. However, one challenge only begets another, and the only way forward is through a commitment to mutual respect and understanding.

I hope you've found this guide to the reality of what's going on in China to be fascinating and educational. Personally, I have dedicated the past two decades of my career to China and have had only positive experiences in business and have formed deep, lifelong friendships with the people of China. What you've read reflects what I have learned in my journeys. Much of it is subjective, but all of it is grounded in fact. That's the past, though. What does the future hold?

Let's look ahead in the last chapter.

CHAPTER FIFTEEN
The Future

I hope you all now see what I found so fascinating and exciting about China, from my Beyoncé and Mick Jagger days to introducing global investors to the growth of China. And, of course, I've barely scratched the surface of all that's going on in one of the world's fastest-growing and dynamic economies. For those interested in comprehensive studies, there are plenty on the KraneShares and CICC websites, as well as countless other sources. If this book does nothing else, I hope it inspires you to take the initiative and explore China yourself.

Whether as an investor, scholar, or visitor, these pages should serve as a guide for where to look. What you find is up to you. I recommend that everyone visit China and experience firsthand the amazing developments across the country and have the opportunity to meet the wonderful people.

As we near the end of this journey, let's briefly look forward.

Pursuing the China Dream has lifted hundreds of millions of people from poverty, enabled many families for the first time to enjoy vacations, an automobile, a nicer house, access to a good education and health care, and more. It's allowed many to advance to the middle class and beyond.

This trend will not only continue but accelerate. Government backing plus an ample source of finance, plus massive infrastructure spending, plus life-changing technology, plus growing access to the rest of the world is a formula for growth. More and more of China's people will be able to live the dream.

And as we've seen in so many areas, this means more opportunity for everybody, including investors who wish to own a part of this growth. This trend will continue, and at some point, it will be as easy, and as safe, to invest in Shanghai as it is in New York.

There will also be tremendous opportunity to satisfy the sophisticated tastes of increasingly wealthy and connected Chinese consumers for everything from video games to Taylor Swift songs to single malt whiskey. Yes, trade is thorny, but it's ultimately win-win. So is tourism, and the Western cultural and entertainment sites that make an effort to cater to tourists from China will be well rewarded. So will local sites in China that invest in infrastructure to welcome guests from home and abroad.

China has made it a national goal to reduce the pollution that can still affect major cities on a bad day, and I'm sure they will succeed. Again, the combination of willpower, plenty of funding, and technological innovation will ultimately prevail. Tied closely to this, as we've seen, is caring for the health of a huge and aging population. I am optimistic.

I'm constantly amazed at the advances I see in smartphones, electric cars, high-speed trains, the ease of shopping, and the burgeoning consumer choices every time I visit. I can't even imagine some of the things that are on the way.

What I'm not surprised about is the amazing accomplishments and transformation I've seen over the past two decades in China. The China Dream is real and beneficial to so many.

I find it difficult to make predictions, but I will make one: The China Dream will lead to more prosperity for more people than we can ever imagine.

ENDNOTES

CHAPTER ONE

1. Henry Kissinger, *On China* (New York: Penguin Books, 2011).
2. GDP data from the World Bank.
3. Henry Kissinger's comments were delivered to the author at a private event in New York City in 2018.
4. Smartphone ownership data from Statista as of December 31, 2019. Retrieved December 18, 2020.
5. Speech by Xi Jinping in Seattle in 2014. Full text available from the National Committee on U.S. China Relations.
6. Based on China's 2019 total population of 1.398 billion, according to the World Bank. Retrieved December 18, 2020.
7. Lu Mai, *The Chinese Dream and Ordinary People* (New York: Springer, 2021).
8. Data from the World Bank.
9. Ray Dalio, "Looking Back on the Last Forty Years of Reforms in China," LinkedIn, January 3, 2019.
10. Caixin Summit, November 14, 2020.

CHAPTER TWO

1. Interview with Kevin Liu, June 27, 2019.
2. https://news.gallup.com/file/poll/331160/210301CountryRatings.pdf.
3. Henry Kissinger's comments were delivered to the author at a private event in New York City in 2018.
4. www.beltroad-initiative.com, retrieved Aug. 10, 2021.
5. "The Belt and Road Initiative: Country Profiles," HKTDC.com as of December 31, 2020.
6. Data from MSCI as of December 31, 2020.
7. Data from MSCI as of December 31, 2020.
8. Documents.worldbank.org, retrieved August 9, 2021.
9. Smartphone ownership data from Statista as of December 31, 2019. Retrieved December 18, 2020.
10. Data from Statista, retrieved August 9, 2021.
11. Steven Lee Myers, "China's Pledge to Be Carbon Neutral by 2060: What It Means," *New York Times*, December 4, 2020.
12. McKinsey data quoted by healthcareglobal.com, retrieved August 9, 2021.

CHAPTER THREE

1. https://KraneShares.com/top-5-reasons-a-win-win-relationship-with-china-benefits-the-us-economy.
2. Data from WHO retrieved August 9, 2021.
3. "In the Face of Lockdown, China's Ecommerce Giants Deliver," hbr.org, retrieved August 9, 2021.
4. Charles McGrath, "Institutions Own 80% of Equity Market," *Pensions & Investments*, April 25, 2017.
5. Dian Zhang, "US Exported Millions in Masks and Ventilators to China in Response to the Coronavirus Crisis," *USA Today*, April 2, 2020.

6. Christina Alesci, "Billionaire Brooklyn Nets Owner Joe Tsai Donates Ventilators and Masks to New York," CNN Business, April 4. 2020.
7. Liza Lin, "China Seeks to Ease Medical Goods Shipment Delays with New Rule," *Wall Street Journal*, April 26, 2020.
8. Trefor Moss, "Neither Coronavirus Nor Trade Tensions Can Stop U.S. Companies' Push into China," *Wall Street Journal*, May 19, 2020.
9. https://www.chathamhouse.org/2021/02/beijings-vaccine-diplomacy-goes-beyond-political-rivalry.
10. "By the Numbers: China Lays Out Ambitious Five-Year Targets," Bloomberg, March 8, 2021.
11. Data from Bloomberg as of December 22, 2020.
12. "2021 China Outlook: Full Speed Ahead," KraneShares.com, retrieved August 9, 2021.
13. Data from Statista, December 2020.
14. Dan Strumpf, "US vs. China in 5G: The Battle Isn't Even Close," *Wall Street Journal*, November 9, 2020.
15. "China's Digital Plan Will Help It Leapfrog US as Tech Leader," *Nikkei Asia*, June 11, 2020.
16. Steven Lee Myers, "China's Pledge to Be Carbon Neutral by 2060: What It Means," *New York Times*, December 4, 2020.
17. www.nrn.com, retrieved August 9, 2021.
18. "The Emerging Middle Class in Developing Countries," oecd.org, retrieved December 9, 2021.

CHAPTER FOUR

1. www.chinacheckup.com, retrieved August 9, 2021.
2. Tracxn.com, retrieved August 9, 2021.
3. www.cbinsights.com, retrieved August 9, 2021.
4. China's Fourteenth Five-Year Plan pdf, cset.georgetown.edu, retrieved August 9, 2021.
5. "By the Numbers: China Lays Out Ambitious Five-Year Targets," Bloomberg, March 8, 2021.

6. "Alibaba's Singles Day Breaks Record," www.practicalecommerce.com, retrieved August 9, 2021.
7. CICC proprietary research used with permission.
8. Celeste Goh, "Lufax IPO a Bright Spot Among Battered Digital Lender Stocks," *S&P Global*, November 27, 2020.

CHAPTER FIVE

1. Data from National Bureau of Statistics of China, December 31, 2015.
2. Data from Statista, retrieved August 11, 2021.

CHAPTER SIX

1. https://KraneShares.com/resources/presentation/2018_12_31_obor_presentation.pdf.
2. "How Big Is China's Belt and Road?" csis.org, March 31, 2019.
3. "Meeting Asia's Infrastructure Needs," adb.org, retrieved August 9, 2021.
4. www.beltroadinitiative.com.
5. "China Renews Its Belt and Road Push for Global Sway," *New York Times*, January 15, 2020.
6. "Gansu Province: Golden Corridor to the Digital Silk Road," www.kraneshares.com, March 30, 2019.
7. "Wanda to Invest 45 Billion Yuan in a Cultural Tourism Project," interpark.co.uk, March 31, 2019.

CHAPTER SEVEN

1. Knoema.com data, retrieved August 11, 2021.
2. KraneShares.com, January 27, 2021.
3. "Jack Ma's $290 Billion Loan Machine Is Changing Chinese Banking," Bloomberg, July 27, 2019.

CHAPTER EIGHT

1. CICC proprietary research. Used with permission.
2. "A Journey to the New Heart of Urbanization in China," kraneshares. com, August 15, 2017.
3. "The Chinese Central Government's State Council Decides to Build the Xiong'an New Area," *Xinhua News*, April 1, 2017. Note: Title translated from Chinese.
4. "The Hype About China's Newest City," *The Economist*, April 12, 2017.
5. "The Chinese Central Government's State Council Decides to Build the Xiong'an New Area," *Xinhua News*, April 1, 2017. Note: Title translated from Chinese.
6. U.S. Census Bureau, "Quick Facts for New York City, New York," retrieved July 14, 2017.
7. "Remarks by President Obama and President Xi of the People's Republic of China in Joint Press Conference," The White House, Office of the Press Secretary, September 25, 2015.
8. World Bank, China demographic data. Retrieved July 17, 2017.
9. Data from the World Bank. Retrieved June 28, 2017.
10. Wei Ge (1999). "Chapter 4: The Performance of Special Economic Zones." Special Economic Zones and the Economic Transition in China. World Scientific Publishing Co Pte Ltd. pp. 67–108.
11. "This 60 Minutes Video of China's Ghost Cities Is More Surreal Than Anything We've Ever Seen," *Business Insider*, March 3, 2013.
12. John Kasarda, Ph.D, "Zhengzhou Takes Off," *Airport World*, September 30, 2016.
13. "Stephen Roach Has Rational Explanation for all of China's Ghost Cities," *Business Insider*, August 29, 2012.
14. https://macropolo.org/digital-projects/high-speed-rail/introduction.
15. Marketsandmarkets.com, Smart Cities Forecast to 2025.

CHAPTER TEN

1. "Spirits, Fashion, Food, Appliances, and the Power of Chinese Consumers," kraneshares.com, February 11, 2021.
2. Mark Macdonald, "One Chinese Liquor Brand Has Become the Life of the Party," *International Herald Tribune*, July 3, 2012.
3. "Spirits, Fashion, Food, Appliances, and the Power of China's Consumer," kraneshares.com, February 11, 2021.
4. "Facial Recognition Is Used in China for Everything from Refuse Collection to Toilet Roll Dispensers and Its Citizens Are Growing Increasingly Alarmed, Survey Shows," *South China Morning Post*, January 27, 2021.
5. https://www.forbes.com/sites/brendanahern/2019/11/11.
6. https://kraneshares.com/q2-china-internet-star-pinduoduo-visits-kraneshares.
7. https://kraneshares.com/china-internet-sector-expanding-despite-trade-tensions.
8. *Hollywood Reporter*, December 1, 2017.

CHAPTER ELEVEN

1. "Remarks by President Xi Jinping at Climate Ambition Summit 2020," xinhuanet.com, retrieved August 9, 2021.
2. https://kraneshares.com/tesla-beyond-a-holistic-approach-to-electric-vehicles-future-mobility-ecosystem.
3. Ihsmarkit.com, retrieved August 9, 2021.
4. Fred Lambert, "China Boosts Electric Car Sales by Removing License Plate Quotas," Electrek, June 6, 2019.
5. Mckinsey.com, retrieved August 9, 2021.
6. "Solar and Wind Cheapest Sources of Power in Most of the World," Bloomberg, April 28, 2020.
7. https://resources.solarbusinesshub.com.

CHAPTER TWELVE

1. "China's Health Care System Uncovered Online Medicine and Beneficiaries of the COVID-19 Pandemic," kraneshares.com, May 11, 2020.

2. "Beyond Coronavirus: Positive Prognosis For China Healthcare Sector," kraneshares.com, March 5, 2020.

3. https://kraneshares.com/resources/presentation/2019_09_30_kure _presentation.pdf.

4. HealthCareAsia, August 10, 2020.

5. www.iqvia.com.

6. www.ispor.org.

7. "China's Health Care Listings Break Record," Wall Street Journal, November 12, 2020.

CHAPTER THIRTEEN

1. "China Sees Sports as Growth Driver After Its Olympics Success," Bloomberg, August 6, 2021.

2. https://www.iaapa.org.

3. Statista.com.

4. National Bureau of Statistics as of December 31, 2019.

5. "An Interview with Investor Relations at Bilibili," kraneshares.com, July 9, 2020.

CHAPTER FOURTEEN

1. Daniel H. Rosen and Lauren Gloudeman, U.S. Chamber of Commerce and Rhodium Group, "Understanding US-China Decoupling: Macro Trends and Industry Impacts," February 17, 2021.

2. "Top Five Reasons a Win-Win Relationship with China Benefits the U.S. Economy," kraneshares.com, June 26, 2020.

3. "Trends in US Multinational Enterprise Activity in China, 2000-2017," uscc.gov.

4. Isis Almeida, "China Steps Up U.S. Soybean Buying with Million-Ton Purchase," Bloomberg, May 11, 2020.

5. https://www.forbes.com/sites/brendanahern/2020/06/24/top-5-reasons-a-win-win-relationship-with-china-benefits-the-us-economy.

6. "The Future of the US-China Relationship & Its Impact on China's Internet Sector," kraneshares.com, December 15, 2020.

7. https://kraneshares.com/perception-versus-reality-on-trade-and-chinas-economy.

8. "Who You Gonna Call?" *The Economist,* July 17, 2021.

9. "Pork Firm Smithfield Sold to China's Shuanghui for $7.1 Billion," *Los Angeles Times*, May 29, 2015.

10. CNBC.com, May 28, 2017.

11. https://kraneshares.com/a-deeper-look-at-us-china-trade-mainland-performance.

12. kraneshares.com/notes-from-KraneShares-china-insights-briefing-with-dr-henry-kissinger.

13. "The Next Chapter in US-China Relations: A Diplomat's View," kraneshares.com, June 17, 2021.

14. "Tariffs and the Economic Marriage of the US and China," kraneshares.com, August 9, 2018.

INDEX

243

ABOUT THE AUTHOR

Jonathan A. Krane is the founder and chief executive officer of KraneShares, an asset management firm delivering China-focused exchange traded funds to global investors. KraneShares focuses on providing expert access and products for investors to gain exposure to China's capital markets. Jonathan has spent the last fifteen years working with companies in China. He previously founded a leading media and entertainment company in China, which was later sold to a publicly traded multinational corporation.

Jonathan received an MBA from Columbia Business School and a BA from Connecticut College. He is a member of the Young Presidents Organization (YPO).